Carolyn Marhbank

THE EXPRESSIVE ARTS

D1150085

Dedicatory poem
(for Seamus Fox)

Because we both believe,
in this materialist night,
there's a logos-light

and because we know
it's in the shapes we make
for human or God's sake

that the light shines through . . .
because we both believe . . .
this one, mate, is for you.

THE EXPRESSIVE ARTS

'Take out the human, and you take out art'
(John Cotton)

Fred Sedgwick

David Fulton Publishers
London

David Fulton Publishers Ltd
2 Barbon Close, London WC1N 3JX

First published in Great Britain by
David Fulton Publishers 1993

Note: The right of Fred Sedgwick to be identified as the author of this work
has been asserted by him in accordance with the Copyright, Designs and
Patents Act 1988.

Copyright © Fred Sedgwick

British Library Cataloguing in Publication Data

A catalogue record for this book is available from the British Library

ISBN 1–85346–200–4

All rights reserved. No part of this publication may be reproduced, stored in a
retrieval system or transmitted, in any form, or by any means, electronic,
mechanical, photocopying, recording or otherwise, without the prior
permission of the publishers.

Typeset by Action Typesetting Limited, Gloucester
Printed in Great Britain by BPCC Wheatons Ltd, Exeter

Acknowledgements

The following friends and colleagues have contributed significantly to this book and I would like to express my gratitude to them: Brigida Martino, Hazel Hollow, Margo Barker, Sandra Redsell, Duncan Allan, Di Brendish, John Mills, Alison Smith, Andrew Pollard, John Cotton, H Burns Elliot, Dawn Sedgwick, Seamus Fox.

Mary Jane Drummond has improved my text with many suggestions, some grammatical, some ideological, some commonsensical – but all of them sound.

Also my thanks are due to the following Suffolk schools: Downing CP, Ipswich; Saxmundham Middle; Woods Loke, Lowestoft; Tattingstone CP, Ipswich; St Helen's CP, Ipswich; Cliff Lane CP, Ipswich; Bramford VCP, Ipswich. Also to Swing Gate First School, Berkhamsted, Hertfordshire.

Abbreviations used

NCC	National Curriculum Council
AMMA	Assistant Masters and Mistresses Association
SEAC	Schools Education and Assessment Council
LMS	Local Management of Schools
CDT	Craft, Design, Technology
INSET	In-Service Education and Training
TVEI	Technical and Vocational Educational Initiative
GRIST	Grant Related In-Service Training

The Author

Fred Sedgwick was a primary headteacher for sixteen years and is now a freelance writer and lecturer, spending much of his time working in schools. He also talks at teachers' centres and colleges, mainly – but not exclusively – on children's writing and poetry. He writes regularly for the *Times Educational Supplement* and other papers. He is co-author (with Sandy Brownjohn) of worksheets on teaching poetry for the Poetry Library at the South Bank Centre, and poetry editor of *Language and Learning*.

Fred Sedgwick's other books are: *The Living Daylights* (poems: Headland 1986); *Here Comes the Assembly Man: a year in the life of a primary school* (Falmer 1989); *This Way That Way* (anthology of poems for children: Mary Glasgow 1989); *Two By Two* (poems for children, with John Cotton: Mary Glasgow 1990); *Lighting Up Time* (on children's writing: Triad 1990); *Lies* (poems: Headland 1992); *Drawing to Learn* (with Dawn Sedgwick: Hodder and Stoughton 1993); *Pizza, Curry, Fish and Chips* (poems for children: Longman, forthcoming).

Contents

'Still Life Still', silkscreen print 1992 by Dale Devereux Barker

Introduction

Curriculum has been nationalised. The concept of public subsidy for the arts is being destroyed. That is the context in which I write, and you could widen it: a newspaper article on my desk says that the original arts report by the National Curriculum Council working party had too much about doing; that seven-year-olds should be able to 'write a simple score'; and that 11-year-olds 'should be able to distinguish elements in Bach's fugue'.

Tomorrow there'll be a letter in the same paper from a group of the most distinguished musicians in Britain saying that the Secretary of State's amendments are going to turn a generation deaf to music by returning to music appreciation, history and empty theorising, and by neglecting the practical joy to be had in making music. I remember music appreciation: Sir putting on *Fingal's Cave* by Mendelssohn, and bored blazered boys being badgered into listening for the waves crashing against the rocks.

The NCC emphasis on speaking and listening is misplaced, a 'right wing think tank' reports in the same paper. There should be more emphasis on 'pencil and paper skills'. The new conservationism spawns Egyptian cutenesses and camp classicisms on the National Gallery, and a Georgian frontage to the new Debenhams in Colchester. The arts reporter in the *Daily Telegraph* writes a column about a TV presenter, Andrew Lloyd Webber and *Joseph and His Amazing Technicolor Dreamcoat*: the presenter's mother, girlfriend and agent wept with joy at his success as he took over the role of Joseph.

Three wise men produce a report which the press hypes as a final back-to-the-basics lurch for primary education. You'd think schools had been working as workshops with sixties happenings

1

going on in them, but most of them have never noticed the sixties, and if standards are falling they're falling because of under-resourcing, demoralisation and confusion caused by too rapid legislation. Or so teachers tell visitors.

This book addresses the issue of the place of the expressive arts in primary schools in the years around and beyond the implementation of the National Curriculum. It comprises a set of case studies on the language arts, painting and drawing, dance and music, that suggest ways forward in teaching these arts to children aged between 4 and 11. It exists not only in an educational context, but in a political and financial one too – hence the sketch above.

The mixture of styles and materials – case record, commentary, illustration, journalism, poems – is meant to suggest the necessarily eclectic way in which teachers and children can respond to the challenge of teaching the arts today. Louis MacNeice talked in his early poem 'Snow' about 'the drunkenness of things being various':

> World is crazier and more of it than we think,
> Incorrigibly plural . . .

and Barthes comments how disorder is preferable to a distorting order. It is indeed more discrepancy, more complexity, more intellectual problems that we need today: not the simplified papers, like DES communications, LEA guidelines and tests that dominate schools. Over-simplification confuses, though I hope I have drawn (as one of Paul Scott's publishers once wrote to him) 'a clear picture of confusion, not a confused picture'.

I have a background in the ethnographic research tradition, which is also anxious about the dangers of over-simplification. So I am concerned with the experience of teachers and children in classrooms, not with statistics or theories. Of course these experiences are subjectively perceived – but this is a strength, not a weakness. And I have frequently worked towards a kind of objectivity in asking questions of other participants in the settings, not just the teachers. I am not concerned with the sort of description of art (or any other educational experience) that takes the child or the teacher out of their normal environment: I am concerned with classrooms, gymnasia, music rooms and halls, and what the human beings in them do.

Statistics are of no value except as footnotes to messy human experience. Theories are generated from living practice: what happens when educational moments are planned, activated and evaluated. Writers who do attempt to set up huge theoretical structures ('Notes towards a pedagogic aesthetic' or 'towards an aesthetic pedagogy') all too often give readers something that bears no relation either to the readers' experiences or to the practice the writer him/herself praises. Theories that begin in massive abstractions are worse than useless: they fog the world where the learning happens.

Thus researchers threaten teachers with theories to show what the teacher should do. Teachers should develop their own theories with each other, and base those theories in collaborative reflection on their own practice. My article 'Chipping at the Monolith' (in *Curriculum* 7/2 1986) presents one case study among many of this happening: an attempt to create a friendly professional environment where innovation is controlled by teachers, and the results belong to them.

Huge attempts at definitions of what art is are also unhelpful. 'Art,' wrote James Joyce, 'is the human disposition of sensible or intelligible matter for an aesthetic end.' The word 'aesthetic' must have to do with matters of taste and beauty, but that takes us no further than Keats' eloquent tautology: ' "Beauty is truth, truth beauty," – that is all/Ye know on earth, and all ye need to know'.

Herbert Read talks of 'pattern informed by sensibility', and Tolstoy writes:

> To invoke in oneself an experience one has once experienced, and having evoked it oneself, then, by means of movements, lines, colours, sounds or forms expressed in words, so to transmit that feeling that others may experience the same feeling – that is the activity of art.
>
> Art is a human activity, consisting in this, that one man consciously, by means of certain external signs, hands on to others feelings he has lived through, and that other people are infected by these feelings, and also experience them.

But the best journalism falls into this definition of art. Koestler requires intellectual illumination (truth) and emotional catharsis (beauty) in any aesthetic experience. Perhaps Marshall McLuhan is right: 'Art is anything you can get away with.' The *Shorter*

Oxford English Dictionary crisply says that 'Art is ... The application of skill to subjects of taste, as poetry, music, etc.'

Art often clashes with the suited, institutionalised culture of the school. One artist in residence made, with the children, a throne from scrap materials, and asked the children to design a background of graffiti. Some of the graffiti did not please the school staff, involving as it did words not in polite use. These words, or some of them, referred to things prominent in the children's and teachers' lives: it is all right that they exist, but not all right that we mention them.

In the case study in this book, Dale Devereux Barker is less concerned with clothes ruined by paint than the schoolteachers are, and *far* less concerned than the parents. What bothers Dale is the exploration in which he, the children and the teachers are engaged. The poet John Cotton has said (in correspondence) 'I write poetry as a form of exploration ... If out of that exploration comes art, that is a fortunate by-product, as it were, but the exploration is of value itself.' Art is like education: it requires an opening out, an increasing of choices, moments of freedom. Art requires risk. Schooling requires training: a closing down. A minimisation of risk.

Art will always challenge the culture's prevailing powers: socially, linguistically, politically, not in all those ways but in one of them. Most schooling avoids such challenges, and it is the arts teacher's difficult job to marry these two conflicting aims. While the school with an artist living in it has to maintain its institutional integrity, it must also honour the exploration of the artist.

The book emphasises poetry and painting at the expense of dance, drama and music. This is because of my own biases. I have been teaching the first two of these subjects intensively for over twenty years. But much of the material in chapters 1–4 on language and visual art is relevant to the chapters on dance, drama and music, because of several factors all the arts have in common: all are under the same threat as society becomes more mechanistic; all celebrate an essential humanity, and relations between human beings; all present similar problems about assessment; and all are essentially aesthetic, in their search, through artistic action and response, for generalised meaning.

They each have a version of a continuum: form/content;

technique/emotion; performance/process; this makes each one worth studying in terms of the others. They each help us in the search for implications of events portrayed. When we cross these implications with vigilant reflection, we edge towards provisional truths that will help us to (as Samuel Johnson put it) 'enjoy and endure'.

Another Samuel – Beckett – said that there was 'nothing to express, nothing with which to express, nothing from which to express, no power to express, no desire to express, together with the obligation to express'. I place this text over my desk because it is the opposite of what Brodsky has called 'graphomania': the desperation to have your name on a book, what John Cotton calls the 'old Kilroy was here syndrome . . . art as a form of *haute graffiti*'. In its subjugation of self in obligation, Beckett's remark has a rich puritanism that we would do well to bring into our talk of the need for self-expression and targets.

In the language chapters, there is a further bias towards poetry. This is partly because of my interests but also because children learn best about their language by writing in the muscular, cliché-rinsed, reflective way that poetry, more than prose, demands. All the lessons we can teach about writing can be taught most effectively through poetry.

But if we understand 'poem' in its pristine Greek sense of making, creating, we can see why poetry has a position in a book like this of almost prototypal significance. Arguably it is language, the word, *logos*, that makes us human; and making artefacts in language that are conscious of their shape, that are reflexive, is the premier aesthetic activity. So Danielle's poem 'Six ways of looking at a torch' stands at the beginning for good reasons: poetry's prototypal status is one, and the other is the fact that the arts are about other ways of looking, and no doubt there are still more ways undreamed of yet in our philosophies.

It is what R S Thomas calls, throughout his work, 'the machine' that mostly threatens the arts and our humanity in modern society. Much as the money-changers are in the educational temple, the arts are being reduced to the level of entities that can be measured in terms of cost-effectiveness. Thus drama is all too often reduced to the pitiful level of training in life skills. Painting becomes the design of posters to exhort children not to chuck litter on the floor, and the posters are (as Duncan Allan – see chapter 3 – said to me) just more litter.

Often, less grossly, art is used as the servant of other subjects. Again, Duncan Allan points out the effects this can have: art is painting shields for Viking ships, and make sure they are perfect circles (oh, good, we've got some maths in there as well). Or it is constructing scenery for yet another production of a fashionable rock opera.

If children are to come to terms, in some provisional way, through art, with universal truths – but seen in their own practice and reflection on that practice – we must resist society's emphasis on money: on usefulness interpreted in purely market-place terms. And we must also resist a tendency for the arts to become mere components in combined courses.

Art teaching is a vital theme if we believe that the arts provide a way of making a critique of society and its way of dealing with human beings, if we believe that the arts enable us to come to a provisional understanding of ourselves, the world and our relations with it. It was this sort of idea that persuaded Yeats that 'the supreme theme' was 'Art and Song'.

Not everyone agrees about the primacy of art in education. David Constantine, in an article in *The Guardian* (15 August 1990) went so far as to say that the teaching of the arts in an age seduced by managerial and mercantile objectives was necessarily an 'opposing exercise'. For Constantine it is clear that both the teacher and the artist (and, above all, one might add, the teacher of the arts) must entertain a view of humankind that is more elevated than that held by, say, the editor of *The Sun*.

Thus, in a mercantile age, when everything – even our health and education – have to be subjected to what a schools minister has called 'the discipline of the market', the arts have a powerful political implication. Understanding and criticism will be valued to the extent to which the arts are valued. In a society where education devalues the arts, clear inferences may be drawn about the importance of democracy in that society. Such a society is cynical in Lord Darlington's sense: it knows the cost of everything and the value of nothing. It is a society where news bulletins will feature daily the share price index, but only monthly the unemployment figures.

And that devaluation can be itemised with depressing rep-etition. The core subject structure in the national curriculum set up a hierarchy that gave the lie to government rhetoric about balance and wholeness. AMMA reported in February

1990 that 'A recent post of education and community worker with a national orchestra found 20 per cent of its applicants were teachers, and teachers proposing to take a drop in salary, too.'

Presumably those teachers wondered what weighting governors and other managers of schools would give the arts when there was always the safe option of the foundation subjects. That option would all too readily soak up any INSET resources. They presumably felt, too, that any schools without a strong commitment to the arts wouldn't be encouraged to increase it in the world of cost effectiveness.

Also, the arts are concerned with experimentation, with the pushing of boundaries forward. Or, as 11-year-old Tulani said to me, with being 'different'. They are what Raymond O'Malley says poetry is: 'the advancing coalface, the point of growth' (in Denys Thompson's collection of essays *Directions*, 1969). This is, of course, an over-simplification. All art needs two facets: the part of it we already know, that risks cliché and stereotype, and the part that O'Malley means, always pushing forward, that knows it's working only when it risks the disapproval of, say, the *Daily Mail*.

If the forward pushing happens without the knowledge of the 'plagiarising' edge (to use Barthes' term) there will be a sense of enormous dislocation, of meaninglessness. But if we rely on the already known, art will degenerate into a decorative imitation of something from the past. This is what is happening with so much post-modernist architecture: witness the Egyptian quaintnesses and the Ionic pillars of the Sainsbury extension to the National Gallery that support an architect's ego and a prince's prejudices as much as they support a shapeless roof.

This book is also watchful of another effect of a mercantile age: sponsorship. Schools that owe funding to a commercial concern are less likely to experiment, and more and more likely to rely on safer arts, like brass band music. A school play that questions the justice of the hegemony of big business will not be produced in a climate that has seen the end of public subsidy. It is easy to predict a time when tobacco firms sponsor plays only if their products are used on stage.

This book's heart is warmed by sentiments of Auden's to the effect that the mere making of art is a political act. While artists work, creating what they think they should make, they tell Management something managers need to be told, often: that the managed are human beings, not numbers. Another view (which, like society's current obsession with money, devalues the arts) suggests that the arts have a basically decorative function. This is the cultural view implicit in most of society's comments about, and actions in, the arts. It gives the arts slight educational functions – it is, in fact, more concerned with training – and links certain of the arts – the plastic especially – to the craft movement, rather than to exploration and discovery.

Though it has no credibility in university departments, the decorative view of the arts is prevalent among writers and readers of escapist fiction. 'These stories are successful,' a writer of romances said on the radio recently 'because life for most of us is mundane.' An escapist view of the arts accepts this mundanity without question. Most poetry written (though not most published) does too: 'The marble domed tomb opens. The world ends ...' The writer hopes that the ersatz drama, the Caspar David Friedrich resonance of lines like that will substitute for learning: the search for the centre in the full knowledge that the search will be ultimately fruitless.

Structuralist theory has accepted texts as of equal significance. After all, *Pride and Prejudice* and an advertisement for corn-flakes are essentially both texts. But experience tells us about differences; and the differences become evident when we ask ourselves whether a text is intended to help us escape or learn, whether it is, in Elaine Moss's vivid terms, 'battery' – like a reading scheme or pulp fiction – or 'free range': a book that works on several levels (quoted in *After Alice*, edited by Morag Styles and others).

There are, of course, other views of the arts implicit in society's dealing with them. One of the most powerful might be termed 'the Grecian Urn view'. This sees the arts as objective creations, and according to this view, the only possible human relationship with them is one of worshipful awe.

The Grecian Urn view effectively disempowers human beings by making art a thing that is beyond their reach: art as an unravished (and unravishable) bride. It legitimates a hierarchy composed of the human beings who are closest to the Urn; who then decide what is genuine knowledge *about* the Urn; thus taking to themselves enormous power in education, through, for example, examination systems; and then the rest of us, who can only gain access to the Urn via the experts, 'the small minority ... the few who are capable of unprompted, first-hand judgement ... Upon this minority depends our power of profiting by the finest human experience of the past ... Upon them depend the implicit standards that order the finer living of the age'.

This resounding summary of the elitist view of art, that sees access to it as only through a body of high priests who can 'discriminate' comes from the highest priest of all, F R Leavis (*Mass Civilisation and Minority Culture* 1930).

Another view of art sees art on the cusp of two centuries, the twentieth and twenty-first, as returning to traditional values. In his book *Living Powers*, Peter Abbs attacks modernism and progressivism as exhausted, even though, as he says, modernism depended on tradition. But he also says that modernism is defined negatively by its opposition to traditional culture.

Eliot, with his obsession with Christianity, Jacobean drama and Sanskrit (to name three traditional influences on that cold, fertile mind) was bathed in the old. Joyce could not have written a word of *Ulysses* without his knowledge of the Greek myths, or a word of *A Portrait of the Artist as a Young Man* without a profound knowledge of (and, of course, confrontation with) the Catholic myths. And Picasso knew the drawing of Raphael better than most anti-modernists.

Modernism has built a massive interactive mechanism which makes the readers of poems, the observers of pictures and the listeners to music conspirators in the act of creation. To do without that insight, we would be back with the Grecian Urn and escapism. Modernism also revitalises our concept of tradition; and the progressive movement, embodied in teachers and thinkers like Caldwell Cook, Montessori, Susan Isaacs and Herbert Read, gave the child some tenuous hold on the processes of his or her education. I work in a version of that tradition that sees both children and teachers as active learners. I'm also sure that children should be exposed to art of the past, from all cultures.

Discussion of education in the nineties has been and will be informed by political decisions of the past few years. For example, the first publications of the National Curriculum, offering, as they do, no space to the arts, gave rise to speculation (pessimistically) that the arts are to have no place or (optimistically) that the searching role of the arts is to be seen in maths,

English and (probably more vitally) science. But this book does not rely on the structures of the National Curriculum which, in its present form, will not, in the future, be as unchangeable as it seems today (early summer 1992) to many teachers.

Also, the book addresses problems of evaluation and assessment, which, as systematically or traditionally conceived, offer nothing to the teaching of the arts. Assessment that is constantly aware of the essentially human – and, therefore, messy – reality will have to be developed if we are not to devalue the arts and our understanding of them with checklists. Brigida Martino, in chapter 6, expresses this difficulty. Mary Jane Drummond's book in this series, *Assessing Children's Learning*, puts this point forcefully, and I accept her humanistic model here.

The most important aspects of education in any subject – coming to terms with Shakespeare, learning about love and sex, coping with bereavement, understanding ecology – all these are simply unmeasurable, and immeasurable. This is not to say they can't be evaluated, but that evaluation has to take into its account the complexity, the emotion, the untidy humanity of these facets of education: the drunkenness, in those immaculate words of MacNeice's, of things being various.

Similarly, to subject my son (I personalise the argument here deliberately) to arithmetical measurement is to devalue him. He said to me when he was five: 'How do they know the universe began with a big bang when there weren't any scientists around, not even dinosaur scientists?' If an assessment system is to mean anything it has to cope with the linguistic complexity in the thought processes of that five-year-old boy. What will other tests identify? Success and failure with reading texts like 'Roger ran' are easy to measure, but such a sentence is dangerously limiting.

Arguably the central question will be whether a pedagogical view of the arts can be taught. We certainly use other entities, like books and magnifying glasses, to help children to learn. Perhaps the arts have an analogous position to these. In teaching the arts, we are teaching children research methods, because each artistic act is an act of research, an investigation into the discrepancy or correspondence between our own perceptions and those of the other human beings around us.

Teaching art, then, is teaching research. It is teaching, as John Cotton has said, exploration. As a poet, he writes 'as a way of exploring what I experience, and what I think and feel about that experience. I explore my emotions and attitudes and of course, the language in which I express them' (*Contemporary Poets* 1991). We have to demonstrate in our teaching 'the holiness of the heart's affections' and offer children the tools for the job: techniques, materials, time, support. This has implications for the teacher, who will have a different status in the classroom, as she or he becomes an enabler, or a resource, as she/he forsakes, increasingly , the altar position behind the desk. The teacher becomes a leader in a community of artists, and, come to that, scientists, technologists, mathematicians.

The notion of reflective professional depends to a large extent on ideas of action research (see especially Lawrence Stenhouse, *An Introduction to Curriculum Development* 1976). The notion of children as active learners will refer back to Piaget, Hadow, Plowden, and numerous other thinkers about education. There is simply no point in deferring to views of children as empty vessels. Children will be active, whatever we do to them. If we want to push their activity, their creativity, on to the playground, we can do that. But we'd better watch out, because it will burst out somewhere.

Brian Way has written of how theatre is concerned with communication between actors and audience, and drama is concerned with the participants' experience. All the arts have that dichotomy built into them. This book is concerned more with the process by which children learn about themselves, the world around them, and the relationship between those two entities than it is about performance, or product; though products may turn out to be what Robert Frost called poems: 'temporary stays against confusion'.

There is a bridge between what children experience in schools as tyro learners about the arts, and what mature artists experience. The common experience is aesthetic. It is finding the difficult point between, on the one hand, attending to, working on, analysing the emerging piece of art, and, on the other, allowing the work of art to work on us, whether we are children, experienced artists, or teachers.

In other words, are we active in an obvious way, or active in being passive, in a kind of attentive waiting. We must let the Holy Spirit, or the Muse, or the subconscious, have its way with us (to use Jorge Luis Borges' elegant formulation, described in *Poetry Dimension* 1975). But to break the rules, you must know about the rules, and that is why my position here is not contradictory to the argument that the most rewarding way of encouraging the making of art is formal. Indeed, rules are necessary in all aesthetic endeavour.

Training ('to exercise, practise, drill' defines the Shorter Oxford English Dictionary) is something else, and it can have no helpful role in teaching a child anything about creating in the field of any of the arts, if the art is about the process of education. Training is only about products; it is unconcerned with the stream through which we painfully and enjoyably wade as we learn.

Education has the function of increasing, while training has the function of decreasing the possibilities that emerge when we play with our environment. Training and education are quite distinct. Training determines. Education explores.

In these terms, teaching the arts is essentially educational, because it must, by definition, increase the range and scope of this search through possibilities. Teaching handwriting would be a suitable example of training, offering, as it does, 'determinate fields of action'.

Stenhouse and his allies in the curriculum evaluation movement won the battle against objectives and targets in the seventies. He was able to point out how they would not cater for learning in the areas where there were serious questions to be asked; that they tended, therefore, to narrow learning to the odds and sods that can be measured; that they tended, because of that tendency, to make teaching banal. He won the battle intellectually. But politically we are now surrounded by the constraints built by objectives, the cash nexus and a lower view of the potential of humankind than is strictly honourable.

For the artist a temporary incoherence is better than an order that shapes, but mis-shapes. The artist understands that his or her work is in some way the articulation of what is hidden, the bringing into the open of which may cause anxiety, discomfort or even revolution, whether of an emotional or political kind. There are earthquaking potentialities in all the arts with which no management style will be comfortable.

But if we are going to educate rather than merely train our pupils, we can't do without them.

CHAPTER 1

Six Ways of Looking at a Torch

Poetry's unnat'ral; no man ever talked poetry 'cept a beadle on boxin' day. (Mr Weller in *Pickwick Papers*)

The first part of this chapter is an account of the writing of a poem.

Of course, that sentence immediately begs a huge question. According to the poet Vernon Scannell, children can't write poems because they haven't the necessary technique or experience: he says, in *A Proper Gentleman*, his delightful account of a poet's residency in an Oxfordshire town, that very young children do not write poems; that to make a poem 'demands intelligence, imagination, passion, understanding, experience and not least a knowledge of the craft'.

It all depends on what you mean by poem. Scannell must be thinking of the dictionary definition 'verbal artefacts of a high order' — though there is clearly no objective account anywhere of what is a high or low order. Perhaps, in his phrase 'knowledge of the craft', he is really defending the territory he and his colleagues have staked out for themselves. Indeed, 'craft' sounds slightly masonic. It's for us to know and for you to find out – if you can.

Stillman, in his ever-useful introduction to his *Poet's Manual and Rhyming Dictionary*, offers a more inclusive definition than Scannell implies. After saying that verse is 'composition in words that employs deliberate patterns of sound', he goes on: 'Poetry ... transcends verse in a way that has escaped definition ... [it] seems to partake of the miraculous ... it adds up to more than the sum of its parts.'

In what follows, I admit that the definition of 'poem' is less than fully dealt with, as I try to tease out what children learn

13

as they write in a purposeful and intense way. Indeed, at times, during work for previous articles on the teaching of poetry, 'poem' has seemed most helpfully defined at least partly in terms of learning – and not just by teachers. As the Czech poet and scientist Miroslav Holub has put it, 'when I write a poem I do an experiment with a yes or no answer'. Writing a poem is about exploring, hypothesising, making little temporary resting places that give us pause in our frightened contemplation of our predicament. There is something miraculous in this, and the same is true for all art. Each painting, each dance, each drama, each composition says 'So I am here. Where next?'

So I define poetry – and all art – as a teacher; the only teacher, Shaw commented somewhere, except torture. But my research into the entries to a national young people's poetry competition ('The Sifter's Story', in *The Cambridge Journal of Education*, 1988) suggests that 'poem' is mostly defined by teachers as a harking back, through rhyme and archaic diction, to a sentimentally viewed past. Thus entries used rhyme, obscurity, quotation, and archaic and foreign references as indispensable conditions; the cultural definition of poetry implied by this exercise was emphatically about honouring a tradition.

And scannings of art society exhibitions, and sittings through amateur dramatic society productions suggest the same is true about the visual and dramatic arts. By contrast, in this case study, a child is experimenting, with her feelings, with the world around her, and with her language. Most of my early notes for what follows were made when I was Danielle's headteacher.

Six way's of looking at a torch

a spot light hitting on the star of our show.
a sense of ice cold apon the world.
the ripple's on the water spalshing on rocks.
the sun with is hipasonik beam.
a spy on the loose looking for a rober.
a pool of blood the shimmer in it.
a golden morning that cant wate to begein
a robot when hes spoted his enamy the light sudden flash's on.
a bandit running on the streets loose
a mass of coulers in a worl to make a gold couler
a silver ring lost reapet again in the light

a horomove moon showing up on every one
a holiday sun not in England this year
a mase of street's I know hes here some were
a dico as the light's flicer on and off
a help gaget all way's ready to help unles the batary's have run down.
a colarge just finished
a sad face with tear's running dawn
a holow tree just wating to be choped down
a sound fadeing away in the disdence
a pair of eye's blue green yellow
a spainish doll danceing

Using a suggestion of Sandy Brownjohn's (in *Does It Have to Rhyme?*) I had tried to demonstrate to children that there is more than one way of looking at something. Brownjohn uses Wallace Stevens' sequence of short lyrics *Thirteen ways of looking at a blackbird*. I held objects up, and showed how different they looked viewed from different angles: spider plant, shell, a bit of a car engine, a mirror. The children quickly saw the freedom this gave them to use words they may well not have used before. The shell, said someone, was like 'a cat curled up by the fire'. 'From behind,' wrote someone else in her notebook, 'the mirror is nothing at all.' And another: 'the cauliflower is a brain'. Danielle began writing with a frenetic speed that it is visible in her rough draft.

This was her tenth poem written with me. She was then a nine-year-old girl brimming with verbal ideas, which sometimes flowed all too prolifically from her, rich and unconsidered; colourful and well-lit, but ill-defined and formless. In the classroom, despite an occasional act of apparently not listening, once my preamble is over, it rapidly emerges that Danielle has been paying sufficient attention. You can tell from her writing. One foggy morning she had behaved in her usual half-present way as I tried to use the weather to capture the class's imagination. She wrote (corrected version):

I pull the steel trap.
Step to find
a cold whisp shudder of mist.
The white flour is lumpy and cold and not
to taste. Pours out before me.
The freeze melts my face

but no water lies at my feet
It's a white mirror you cannot touch.
Your brain drops out of your forehead with pain.
Your hand disappears in the light dark.
A tree glimmers still with fright.
An invisible man taps you on your shoulder.
A house, crooked and bent for doves
blends in with the colour of the mist.

Danielle has a different way of paying attention from most children, and I realised suddenly, while attending a lecture on the privatisation of groundstaff in schools, that it was the same as my way. I tune in to what I think I need, and let the rest go hang. I then concentrate on my private thoughts, or a book brought into the room for the purpose, or (on this occasion) a draft of this chapter.

Danielle is also a brilliant disco-dancer, as I've discovered while running money-raising sessions in the school hall at lunchtimes. Her sense of rhythm appears to be perfect, as she sings The Calypso Carol in the front row of the choir, her singing forceful and enthusiastic; her nodding head following the off-beat. This sense of rhythm appears in her writing in a grasp of cadence. Her phrasing is immaculate.

The uncontrolled piece with which I began this chapter was the work of about twenty minutes. Had I known I was going to get so involved, I would have checked all this, like a good number-crunching researcher: how long it took, how she went about the task, whether she talked most of the time, where she was sitting. I'd certainly have kept her manuscript. But all this was merely human life then, not the subject for a chapter in a book. So the details are lost. I just remember Danielle coming to the desk and saying 'I've finished'. I said, after reading the poem, 'This is brilliant, Danielle' or words roughly to that effect and then (at this point the focus shifts from Danielle's writing to my teaching) I corrected some of her mistakes, technical matters of spelling and punctuation. She stood impatiently by me, probably hoping that something more interesting would happen soon, like Adam coming in late, or the secretary looking in the door to call me to the phone, or the class clown, Jeremy, falling off his chair.

I was too quick to correct – almost all teachers are. And if I want to demonstrate how ill-timed technical correction can be,

I can do no better than the following: I originally wrote this on an electric typewriter, and the paper gave me the last two paragraphs like this:

This rather wiuld, uncontrolled piece was the work,of about twenty minutes: if 18d know I was going to get so involved, I'd have checked all, this kind of studff at the time. I said 'This is brilliant, Danielle – let8s look at some of the mistakes ' – and then i went through it, correcting technical errors of spelling and punctuation. She stood impatiently by me, probably hoping something more interesting would happen soon.

I think I was too imediate on this correction thing. I think nearly all teachers are. And if I want to demonstrate this, I need lok no forward that the paper coming out of this typewriter right now: let me give you the last two paragraphs exactly as I typed them first:

I would be impatient if a reader were to respond to those quick-typed words as though I *meant* them. Or rather, as though the crudities of expression, let alone the grammatical mistakes, were what counted, were part of the essential me. In fact, the paragraphs were a netting of something before it escaped. They constituted a draft, and I didn't worry about any technical inaccuracy, nor about any crudities of expression. As Frank Smith says in *Writing and the writer*, 'composing and transcribing ... can interfere with one another'. Where something has to be netted, correct transcribing has to wait for later, whether one is a child writing in the classroom or an adult working under different pressures in a study.

But because Danielle is a child, I had no worries about homing in, after the first verbal encouragement, on mistakes. I was concentrating on what the National Curriculum Council calls (following Frank Smith) the 'secretarial' side of writing, as opposed to the 'compositional' side. Smith points out that wealthy writers are lucky enough to be able to dispense with this aspect of writing: one thinks of linen-suited novelists and songwriters dictating their work to secretaries; letting them worry about punctuation, spelling and the right keys of the typewriter. The fact that this distinction can be made in writers' lives should alert us to the existence of these two aspects of writing.

I would have said that I was almost entirely interested in the composition of Danielle's work here – but, apart from the bland and unhelpful 'brilliant', *I made all my initial comments on the secretarial side.* This is in defiance of the advice offered by the

National Curriculum Council: 'A measure of tolerance of errors in different language tasks is essential'. Thus, in spite of my rhetoric about expression, I acted as if I was chiefly concerned with communication in its crudest forms; and, indeed, with a purely instrumentalist view of language that sees it as a matter of getting things across to another person after one draft, rather than as a medium of coming to terms with one's own nature and the world that surrounds it through correction and re-drafting; through second and third thoughts; through the reflection on ideas that drafting encourages.

This is a result of my socialisation as a teacher. We all want something now: to display, to show to a parent, to tick off on a National Curriculum derived checklist. But we had better face up to the fact that this socialisation is anti-educational, at least in this example. If we want children to learn through their writing, we should leave the 'corrections' until the composition has been finished.

The first category of secretarial corrections was to do with the capital letters and full stops: Danielle had used none of the former, and her conscientious use of the latter had stopped halfway through. I believe this is because, somewhere around this point, her stream of consciousness began bucketing forward at such a rate that secretarial considerations were an irrelevance. The other category was to do with spelling, and her mistakes make a bizarre little lexicon: spalshing, hipasonik, horomove, flicer, colarge, disdence, spainish.

It was only when I'd satisfied myself with the secretarial matters that I looked seriously at the content of Danielle's draft: the sparkling hither/thither gusto of her ideas, the vigour of the verbs: 'running', 'flicker' and so on. My purposeful interest in the inventiveness came long after the secretarial correction. But eventually the energy of the verbs 'running', 'hitting' and 'flicker' decided me on a project I'd not tried before.

I typed Danielle's writing out, fully corrected secretarially, with a few additions (such as 'It's' to change the clauses and phrases into sentences). I also altered some line endings. I went over this with Danielle, in her mother's presence, before school next morning and suggested that she spend some of that day cutting up my typescript of her writing and rearranging it in groups of lines, so that related material was together. If I had put the piece in order, it would have been 'a distorting order' as Roland Barthes puts it; and, as he says, 'incoherence is preferable'. But by offering Danielle the chance to set things more logically, I was also offering her more autonomy over her work than is usual. I wish now I had left the line endings and the sentences to her.

The groups she identified were about: bandits, robots, spies and related ideas; the cold; sounds; bright light and colour generally; and a few miscellaneous things. Danielle seemed unhappy with the idea at first but when I went half an hour later to her classroom she had worked enthusiastically and had nearly finished. A few minutes later her paper was arranged horizontally, with the sentences sellotaped to it in a new order. I typed up this new version. She had a new title:

A spy out and about

It's a bandit running on the streets, loose.
It's a spy out and about
looking for a robber.
It's a maze of streets
– I know he's there somewhere! –
It's a robot
when he's spotted his enemy,
a horror movie showing up on everyone.

It's a sense of ice
cold upon the world,
ripples on the water
splashing on the rocks,
a sad face with tears running down,
a pool of blood, the shimmer in it.

It's a pair of eyes,
blue, red, green, yellow,
a hollow tree
just waiting
to be chopped down,
a sound
fading away
in the distance.

It's a spotlight
hitting the star of our show,

a mass of colours in a whirl
to make a gold colour
or the sun with its hypersonic beam.
It's a disco as the lights
flicker on and off,
a silver ring repeated again and again in the night,
a golden morning that can't wait to begin.

It's a collage just finished,
a help gadget always ready to help
unless the batteries run down.

It's a Spanish doll
dancing.

(*Danielle Price, 14 October*)

The success of the final draft relative to the piece printed at the beginning of this section suggests some benefits that Danielle had gained, and that many children could gain, from this kind of work, that is, from work that emphasises drafting, provisionality, the fact that everything is in a state of flux.

Interestingly, the very technique I was using in this teaching also emphasised a provisionality. If we can look at a torch in six different ways, how many ways can we look at an avowal of friendship, a government statement, a poem, a text from the New Testament or (as Sandra Redsell suggests in chapter 7) a historical event? That lesson in itself is valuable because at a different level it can teach us to honour other ways of looking at bigger ideas: like love, or God, or life itself. Poetry in this context is a way of developing the imagination so that the writer can see things from other people's points of view. The best work is often written when children are specifically asked to look at something from a position not their own; where they are asked for example, to empathise with an old person, or a historical figure, or one of their parents – or even a banana:

Grab me please, grab me, unpeel me quick;
and let me take a dip
into your ghost cave.

I am warm in this skin

I am thin as a pin

and I want to take a dip
in your ghost cave, QUICK.

(*Amanda 10*)

or an apple:

Waiting Waiting Waiting for you
waiting is all I do.

I want you to grab me
hold me fast.

My sweet taste will make you blink.

I will roll like the world in your head.

I will whisk you around till I am tired.

Waiting Waiting Waiting
all I do is wait.

(*Joanne, 8*)

or they can see a familiar image in a new way:

Inside the chestnut-brown garage
coils of metal straw lie on the floor
and mechanical animals stare as if blind.
Mary is clad in a dress shimmering like flowing oil
bending stiffly over the manger – a brown wooden crate.
Inside the crate
sudden screams
like a run-down chain-saw,
the baby, an engine in the making,
flashes its petrol-coloured eyes like rusty cogs,
thrashes its arms around.
Joseph strides over,
a live robot,
and picks up the engine in his arms.
A strong smell of hay and corn,
grit, grime,
not a garage –
a stable.

(*Alison, 11*)

She has looked at the nativity story through the eyes of a motor mechanic – from an idea from Jill Pirrie's *On Common Ground*, now unfortunately out of print.

Work that emphasises provisionality enables children to concentrate on their materials: the words they've drafted and some options. This provides an intense learning experience as it forces them to reflect on language – the appropriateness of some words in terms of their meanings, sounds, rhymes, allusions, when compared to others. In the very act of crossing a word out, they are reflecting on its meaning and its sound.

Danielle's mother, also a teacher, said to me: 'I think drafting and conferencing are brilliant. I found that gradually the less brave children ... spoke up and read their work out. I used to give them a great big piece of kitchen paper to put down their original ideas. They knew that they could add things, cross things out, put in arrows, make spelling mistakes. I set time limits to put down their ideas, followed by reading aloud to a friend ... some time to add things, some time to correct any spellings they think are wrong, using the dictionary.'

This sort of process also makes them think about themselves and whatever it was that made them write what they wrote. We know, of course, what made them write: the teacher. But beyond that, what made them write the words they chose. This is learning about themselves. They are also learning about the process of learning, whether that process is a hard slog or an inspiration or (to be more realistic) a point somewhere in the middle.

Each draft provides a new base-line for learning. A new framing of the material inevitably introduces new material through a freshly-glimpsed chink in the boundaries. For this and other less serious reasons (appearance and style, for example) drafting is part of the process of writing for all of us except in the most casual of tasks, like notes left on going out, for example, or shopping lists. No teacher sends out the first version of a letter applying for a job. No feasibility study goes to the head of section without a long gestation in the word processor, where it changes and grows and become sharper and clearer.

We do not need to be creative artists to realise the need to draft; but there is an artist in all of us, usually sent to sleep early on in our lives by the instrumentalist nagging of the secretary who appears the moment someone says, when we have tried to say something on a piece of paper, 'That could be neater. Have you spelt that right? What about your italic handwriting? You have forgotten we always put the date first, and where is your margin?' Drafting offers the only way into a satisfying form, and I noted after this unusual series of events that I must allow children more chance to play with their material with the kind of freedom that a word processor would offer. Danielle's experience was like the one a word processor offers in that she could re-order her work.

One factor that discourages drafting is the sheer glitter of a first draft like Danielle's. Another is a puritanical obsession with getting jobs done and moving on to the next, rather than staying put and learning some more. Often we say, unpardonably, 'Danielle, that's really lovely. Now can you get on with your maths/science/art.' Another problem with drafting, and its explosion in English teaching over the past ten years, has been that it has been used as yet another tyranny over the child. While before the child had to write only two versions of a good piece of work – the first one and the 'fair copy' to be illustrated marginally and double mounted – now she has to write out several. But this is a serious misunderstanding of drafting, which isn't about reaching an absolute condition of perfection, but about learning through changing.

To economise on boring and unproductive work, several drafts should exist together as children cross things out, write *stet* ('let it stand') when they change their minds, add phrases in loops arrowed to where they want them to go, use oblique lines to work out where line endings might go. They should be discouraged from using erasers, which destroy sentences they might need later, and which imply neatness as the first priority, rather than learning, which is in essence messy. The presence of Tippex in a writer's desk is almost a neurosis. Children draft well after they have played with words and ideas untidily and messily, by reading their work aloud to themselves and to their friends; and by making suggestions for each other's work.

In the case of this piece, I was too concerned with converting the ill-spelt, grammatically unconventional, fraught mix of Danielle's imagery into a correctly-spelt, conventionally grammatical poem. The scissors and sellotape freed us both: Danielle into a better poem, me into an article that is slowly, now, becoming this chapter under my fingers. Though it must be said that Danielle's comments on the re-drafting are less positive:

I didn't mind doing it but I found it a bit boring. I would have changed some of it but not all of it ... I would have put the star bit with the sun bit because they join together. He said "I think 'run down' *not* 'run out'. I put run *out*. I preferred run *out* ... I was pleased with it, but then again I was pleased with my first version ... It's Mr Sedgwick's poem as well as mine really ...'

Something else that stops us encouraging children to learn through this drafting experience is lack of time. There's also the *curriculum interruptus* of the non-integrated day. In many schools children aren't given the time to develop work. 'You're doing well, but now it's time for maths.' And there are, of course, twenty to thirty children in the class. And we know that they get, on average, only two minutes of conversation with their teacher each day. But it is vital that we find ways of offering children this kind of experience, and thereby setting them all off along the road that leads to greater autonomy as writers. What's more, greater autonomy as writers means greater autonomy as human beings. Each of us is entitled to the intellectually muscular experience of drafting, and the implied acceptance of the provisional, because no writing is ever truly complete.

Danielle's ideas run loose on her first notes – 'a spy out and about'. Those ideas, and this child's active imagination, show how deeply she needs the opportunity to collaborate and search for a provisional pattern that will set the world, at least for the moment, in some sort of order. One way of getting over the time problem is to teach the children to help each other make drafts. Here is one approach to the process spelt out:

(1) The children, in a silent period of about twenty minutes, make their initial, exploratory notes. They study them and read them to themselves.
(2) In small self-chosen groups, they read their work to each other, asking questions: Why do you say that? Tell me more about that? What do you mean by ...? They add answers to these questions to their notes.
(3) They redraft, using material that has emerged from the questioning time.

(4) They let their writing 'drain' (to use Kipling's helpful word) and look at it again another day, after they have done something else completely different.

I have treated Danielle's writing as a poem throughout; nevertheless there is a lively debate about whether children are poets at all. On *Desert Island Discs*, Seamus Heaney said that many people are born poets. 'The child is fearful, and that element of fear is vital to a poet's life.' He suggested that as we conquer that fear, that awe about existence, the poetry potential lessens, and in many cases dies.

Robert Hull, in his book *Behind the Poem*, quotes Bing Xin:

> The child
> is a great poet
> with an imperfect tongue
> lisping perfect verses.

To say that a child is a poet we do not need to compare her work to Shakespeare's or Vernon Scannell's to justify our judgement. In fact the comparisons are meaningless. The case for the child-poet is made if we accept that she has had intense experience, is honest, is 'still anxious to get things right' (as Hughes put it), 'still under the primeval dread of misunderstanding the situation'.

The argument, on the other hand, that the notion of the child-poet is sentimental, depends upon the notion of poetry as pre-eminently a matter of form and technique. It is obvious that children haven't conquered these elements to the extent that adults have. But they do have at least a provisional conquest over feeling. And what more could any adult say?

The anti-child-poet argument also uses Touchstone's touchstone. When Audrey asks him whether poetry is 'honest in deed and word? Is it a true thing?' he replies 'No truly; for the truest poetry is the most feigning'. What children lack is, to put it bluntly, the ability to lie in an artistic context, the ability to feign.

What is the difference between poetry and prose? Heaney said that poetry isn't completely tamed yet; the novel and the play are part of the normal social intercourse of our society, whereas poetry still retains parts of the bardic inheritance, the sense that there is magic around, that it is potentially dangerous. Auden knew that poetry is magic, and says so explicitly in the dedication to his *Collected Poems*.

But the fear and anxiety that poetry places, like an asp, on many adult breasts are terrible. I told an education officer who admired my prose book *Here Comes the Assembly Man* that I'd also edited an anthology of poetry for schools, and this (I said) is it. I could almost smell the garlic as he protected his shoulders with the palms of his hands. He said 'I'm afraid I've got a blind spot as far as poetry is concerned'. What causes such defensiveness? What is the power here that makes Mr Suit recoil so unashamedly? I suspect some teacher asked the officer, when he was still in short trousers, to identify the personification, or the metaphor, or the metre, in 'Lycidas': an extreme version of the pr-eminence of form over feeling. Or made him learn a passage from 'Paradise Lost', or 'Elegy in a Country Churchyard' by heart (as we inappropriately put it) on pain (more appropriate, that) of detention.

But more importantly, poetry, as Auden wrote, is sin. It is a primal speech against someone telling you you mustn't do something. It is magic: nasty bothersome stuff. It is a way of saying magic's been done before, and you may do it too if you find your own way of magicking, if you find (as poets say) your own voice.

Picked up gently with these fingers
there's a light in this room.
It moves like Concorde,
it flashes in front of it
blasting like a firework
making its silken surface
glisten and shine
like a star new to the world.
It's gone.
I feel as if I've swallowed a ball.
It's circling in my stomach
like Saturn orbiting the sun.
Suddenly I felt nothing
and there's my glossy glass pyramid
gleaming under the light
of the classroom.

(*Pauline, 11*)

And as Larkin says about desire, where poetry takes charge 'readings may grow erratic'. In the case of this strange poem, this is, roughly what I'd said to a group of eight Y6 children: 'You have something small and very precious in front of you – don't tell anyone, not me certainly, what it is! – and you are looking at it. Decide: What materials is it made of? What shape it is? Is it breakable? What are its colours?

'Now. Pick it up and look at it. Look into it, all round it. Study it, gaze at it. Decide on some words to describe it. Decide where you might keep it. What would you do with it when you're alone ... Write about your precious thing ...'

I asked Seamus Heaney at a reading how he knew when a poem really was a poem, and he said that ultimately it was 'an erotic feeling'. Being mixed up with poetry is a semi-adulterous relationship as Heaney appreciates (see 'An Afterwards' in *Fieldwork*.) It is also unsociable in ways that are less noticeable, less disruptive, less dramatic. It involves, as Larkin noted, a lamp, the noise of wind and 'the moon thinned/To an air-sharpened blade'. Estragon, in *Waiting for Godot*, understood several important things when he replied to Vladimir's 'You should have been a poet' with 'I was' and a gesture towards his rags: 'Isn't that obvious?' Poetry is never about surfaces: clothes that impress or party wit. Maybe that's why Mr Officer Suit is so anxious about it.

Indeed, the *Which?*-conversationalists trust the wind-listeners no more than Caesar trusted lean and hungry looks. They catch sight of that scruffy person in the small room, hunched over a notebook or an Amstrad, and wonder why he or she isn't in the *Which?* marketplace, discussing cameras, carburettors and CD players. They believe 'All solitude is selfish'.

That is why we disempower poetry as often as we can, with notions of 'poetry-love' (I think that I shall never see/A poem lovely as a tree' – a lyric that honours neither trees nor poems). Or we hang silly questions all over poems in textbooks, disguised as helpful textual notes ('What colour are mushrooms? What would they say if they could speak?'). Or we press-gang poetry into agitation and propaganda:

In my back yard I wonder
And in my thoughts I ponder,
Religious racism
It's full of ism and schism ...

(from *Race and Society*, a selection of poems and paintings by school children in Harrow)

All this suggests a cultural view of the difference between poetry and prose. Prose can be read on the beach. Poetry can't. Although with our heads most of us probably agree with Auden when he says 'poetry makes nothing happen', we are not too sure: we are also with seven-year-old Katie who believed a poem might help her get rid of her freckles:

go little brown imps
from my pink hill

go old moles
from my pink hill

go freckles go
from my pink hill

There is probably more chance of that happening than of the world being made non-racist through the agency of a poem.

Danielle moved away to Cumbria. One day two years later a little parcel came through the post. It was a book called ' ... not all lead and fluorspar ...': Stories and poems from Weardale. Gillian Allnut was writer in residence at Danielle's new school, Wolsingham Comprehensive. Danielle had written on the title page with that mixture of formality and informality characteristic of children's letters:

Dear Mr Sedgwick

this is my school book written with Gillian Allnut, My poem is on page 22 and is called 'Brown'.

love Danielle Price.

Brown is the colour of ...
The rustle of dead leaves,
something that has been lost for so long
and now has been found,
a cry of thoughts,
a smell of factory burning sound,
a sound of bruised apple falling to the ground,
a fabulous dragon firing flames of chocolate.
Some park bench in the thought of thoughts,
thousands of maggots eating at a mouldy banana.

It's early autumn when the sun's getting ready for bed,
It's a thousand shells all knocked into one,
It's chestnut tree and the nut is cooked
for the delicious taste,
It's peace and harmony in notes of music,
it's left, right, orders to a soldier,
it's past, knocking on present's door.

The spy was still out and about. She was still looking.

CHAPTER 2

Where is the Age of Nine Gone?

> Gradually I came to know where I was, and I tried to express my
> wants to those who could gratify them, yet could not, because my
> wants were inside me, and they were outside, nor had they any
> power of getting inside my soul. And so I made movements and
> sounds, signs like my wants, the few I could, the best I could;
> for they were not really like my meaning. And when I was not
> obeyed, because people did not understand me, or because they
> would not do me harm, I was angry, because elders did not
> submit to me, because freeman would not slave for me, and I
> avenged myself on them by tears.

That extract comes from St Augustine's recollections of his
childhood. It's a surprising quotation to come across in a
book about the arts in the primary school. It is a surprising
quotation, too, for those of us who have been led to believe
that only post-romantic writers considered it important to try
to understand the mind of a child, and his and her unique
orientation to the rest of the world.

Impressions and feelings

Most of the children in Shakespeare are cyphers, but here is a
writer from the fourth century showing the same concerns as
this book shows: how do we express ourselves, our needs, our
joys, our miseries; how do we make public, appropriately, the
self that seems to be inside us. His words are relevant to our
concerns in this book because the arts, in the context of the
life of a child, can be seen as a passionate attempt to do what
Augustine recalls trying to do as a baby: 'to express my wants
to those who could gratify them'. Artistic frustration is vividly
described later on: 'my wants were inside me, and they were

outside, nor had they any power of getting inside my soul. And so I made movements and sounds, signs like my wants, the few I could, the best I could; for they were not really like my meaning. And when I was not obeyed, because people did not understand me ...'

That's the intolerable struggle, one might say, altering Eliot, of movements and meanings. We make sounds as well, and shapes and patterns that for the moment are just like our meanings. But they go wrong, and are misunderstood. We cannot, as children, make our wants and needs into a publicly understood shape.

Narrative takes many forms. Nostalgia, as here and in the famous vivid passages from Wordsworth's *Prelude*, is a powerful subject if we allow the child full rein to use it:

When I was on holiday last Easter we were staying in a National Trust cottage that had been made into two. In the other half a family called Hall lived. They had lots of boys and one girl. We only played with the girl Sally and the youngest boy Jim. We used to play Kick the Can and my sisters and Sally used to say we [Jim and I] were in love and I used to say they were batty. But I really loved him.

One day Sally said to me 'Did you hear Jim shout "I love you Alison"?' I said 'No' and on the last night my sister said 'Now, that song, "Love is something if you give it away" – why don't you tell it to Jim?' and I said 'OK'.

Jim was in bed so we went downstairs and told him and he smiled and blushed and went down to the bottom of the bed.

Alison has been given an opportunity here to write frankly about an important event. There is something in the atmosphere, the tradition of the classroom that tells her she won't be laughed at for writing in this way. Every classroom needs this micro-tradition if it is to encourage artistic creation; it says, go on, put it down, don't feel embarrassed.

Helen, who was ten, wrote the following after she had heard Wes Magee's poem 'Good Questions, Bad Answers' (from *Island of the Children*, edited by Angela Huth). This piece is another example of a child using the art of narrative to express, to get outside herself, the essence of what it is to be her:

Where is the age of nine gone which somehow I enjoyed being? Down the drain forever.

Where are the shoes with black soles and red bows which I had three years ago? Threw them away.

Where's the bird with the big black beak which did not have a cage and stood on a perch all alone? Sold it.

Where's my golden ringlets that I had in my hair when I was two? Got them cut out.

Where's our old house gone which I moved out of last week? Sold it.

One day my son Daniel, who was seven at the time, ran screaming into the house from the garden. For the first time since his babyhood he was hysterical and inconsolable, and for some time we searched him for an injury, and questioned him about some all too imaginable experience. It turned out that he had seen a ghost. This was the white paint he had on a previous occasion daubed on the inside of the garage wall. We tried, with only partial success, to convince him there were no ghosts in the garage. More than a year later, he wrote this at school:

One day I was painting our shed, I had just started the inside when the paint ran out and it left a mark like a ghost.

Before I painted it, the back was like a black shape, but now instead there was a ghostly white shape.

About a month later I was playing football. I was getting tired so I was walking round to the back door. I could just see the shed.

Suddenly there was a wailing noise coming from the shed. I ran indoors as fast as I could. My heart was in my mouth. I ran to my room. The noise had stopped.

I have found that one way of getting children to write narrative is to ask them to imitate, or partake in, a medium they already know. This is Daniel again, writing a picture book for younger children. It's called *Woofter and Arnold*. Woofter, it is almost clear from the illustrations, is a dog. Arnold is a lion:

One day Woofter was walking in the jungle when Arnold roared and jumped out at him.

Woofter was taken by surprise. He ran like the wind for he had this gift. Arnold soon got tired and gave up.

'That horrible show-off is always ruining my life. I must stop him' thought Woofter.

In the night Woofter banged and hammered. In the morning he had a cage and he was proud of it.

Then he set it with bait which was Arnold's favourite food which was chicken.

When Arnold came he said 'I think this is a trap'. He got some rope and put a spike in the end.

He threw the spike at the meat and pulled it out then he ate it very noisily.

When Woofter came along and found that his trap had failed he spent the rest of the day thinking. Even when Arnold chased him he was still thinking.

He thought all night and in the morning he had thought of plan two.

He made a trip wire which went from a tree and then was nailed to the ground. Up the tree was a big mallet made of wood.

It was done so that if you tripped the mallet would hit you on the head.

When Arnold came along he chased Woofter who walked very slowly over the trip-wire but . . .

Arnold ran into the trip wire and the mallet flew down and hit him on the head.

He was knocked out. When he came round he said 'Where am I' Then he remembered. He looked for Woofter.

But Woofter was asleep in bed.

THE END.

In all these examples we see the power of narrative to help us get closer to terms with the frightening aspects of our lives. Love, the pace of life, those irrational experiences that scare all of us at some time or another, bullying. Using art, in this case narrative, to explore these sensations and experiences gives us a temporary shape to our sufferings, makes them bearable, and enables us to reflect on them in a relatively secure way.

Here is a five-year-old telling a very simple story – but an important one:

When I was angry I smacked my mummy and kicked my mummy and then I went to bed.

Another valuable mode of narrative writing for children is history. Studying history increases our understanding of the past and our ability to cope with the present and future, and children can focus more clearly on history if they are encouraged to use writing. It strengthens our grip over our language.

The following work also demonstrates the value of having writers working in schools. In chapters 3 and 4 Duncan Allan and I describe the impact of the artist Dale Devereux Barker on a school (as well as the school's impact on him). On another occasion, a school brought in the writer Kevin Crossley-Holland to work with a class of Y5 children. He showed the children how writers can be entertaining, and contradicted the world's message that only the brightest visual images count nowadays.

Mum and Dad had been killed . . . Our lovely village, our peaceful village, is just a mass of fire and straw . . . We found another place and now we are happy again.

(*Claire, 9*)

Great sails being lowered. Oars moving in time. The village doomed. The brave men gathered on the shore, but they were all hypnotised. The Danes landed, cutting down the men as if they were already dead, burning everything, everybody dead. But I had hidden. I ran in terror.

I stand by the shore gazing out to sea, speechless as the big black wings creep forward. I think to myself, what shall I do? I shout out 'Danes, Danes!' I am too late. They have landed. I just get away but the others are swept to the ground with their eyes closed. Not a sound left, but I move on.

(*Johnnie, 9*)

These children had spent a day with a writer who knows as much as anyone about the Vikings, and his enthusiasm and knowledge comes through here: note that very Saxon construction 'swept to the ground with their eyes closed'.

Claire's sentimental ending may not be true to the history, but it is a vital part of the piece, and should not be corrected. She has just written the terrible sentence 'Mum and Dad had been killed'. We had invited her to write this ('imagine what it would be like to lose your family in a Viking raid') and therefore we must understand that she will need to end her writing with something that brings things back to a happy normality. That is why Daniel ended *Woofter and Arnold* with 'But Woofter was asleep in bed. THE END.' When children's writing ends 'then they went home, had their tea, and went to bed' it is for a good reason: we can use writing to make ourselves comfortable with our reality. We have to be very sensitive indeed if we are going to correct this sort of trick without distressing a child, which is never a justifiable means to any end in the classroom.

Also, history is not a succession of facts, but an interaction between accounts of events (which may or may not be reliable) and our own reactions to them. So Claire's sentimentalism is to be seen alongside a historian's political bias, or a particular interest in an event that clouds accounts of other events. This point about the eternal subjectivity of historical accounts, is dealt with by Sandra Redsell in her work in drama (see chapter 7).

Here is a seven-year-old girl, Gemma, writing after watching a television programme about Captain Cook:

I was giving out the yucky sauerkraut when one of my friends was shouting out 'Island, Island!' And as he was saying that I came out and I dropped the spoon and the bit of sauerkraut on the spoon went up the walls and on the floor. So when Captain Cook came in I had a little bit of work to do. Then we were on the island and I was shouting 'Hooray Hooray, we will not have to eat that yucky sauerkraut, we can eat some fresh fish'.

It is not the function of this sort of writing (or of our teaching of history to juniors generally) to get bare dates and facts across, but to encourage empathy (as here) with a historical figure's predicament.

Finally on the subject of history, I have always been moved by the story of the *Titanic* – Walter Lord's book *A Night to Remember* is probably the best source for information that I know. Hans Magnus Enzenberger's long poem 'The Sinking of the Titanic', although in effect a metaphor for twentieth-century European history, will also inspire a teacher using this subject for writing.

I told a group of ten-year-olds the story, and asked them to write about it:

The band are playing cheerful notes. It doesn't exactly go with the situation. One bugalist falls overboard and one other stops playing and suddenly runs and jumps overboard. The band keeps playing.
    People are crying, others are trying to commit suicide because their loved ones are dead.
    There's even one man greedy enough to smash a porthole window and get some of the first class passengers' treasures or money.
    There's a sudden yank. The boat goes up almost perpendicular but not quite.
    I fall over and slip overboard, and the water is freezing ...

(Andrew)

In the background I can hear the band playing, people are screaming and shouting and jumping off the deck. I can hear the oars of the boat creaking ... There is a small boy on our boat who is crying his head off because his mother is still on the sinking Titanic for all he knows. The back end of the Titanic is about 65 degrees in the air.

The moon is glinting on the Titanic. The moon is the only light we have. On the horizon we can see the Titanic, it is in chaos by the looks of it ...

(*Robin*)

The boat was pushed away from the Titanic with only ten people in it.

I jumped. I wasn't waiting for the ship to go down. The sea was freezing. I wish I hadn't jumped, instead of drowning I will probably freeze to death ... There was utter confusion, but the band was still playing. People were climbing into life rafts and rowing boats. The posh nobs objected to steerage coming on the boats with them. There were only about nine or ten to a boat.

(*Steven*)

If this writing works, it is at least partly because I was teaching a story that moved me. Other historical figures, situations and events that I use are:

- Helen Keller
- Victorian childhood
- The Guy Fawkes plot
- The trenches in the First World War (using, sometimes, with children I know well, poems by Wilfred Owen and Siegfried Sassoon).

For more on the arts and history see chapter 7 where Sandra Redsell encourages children to empathise with the Vikings, for example, through drama.

Scientific observation

The observation of significant similarities, differences, changes over time and the links between one feature and another, are the starting points for much scientific work ... Hypotheses will often arise from such observations ... These hypotheses will often lead to further investigations. (Non-statutory Guidance in National Curriculum Science)

Car Engine

There's an elephant's trunk hidden under the bonnet!

There's a mass of worms around a large metal heart, it's a shivering shaking heart of a lizard hidden in a mass of secrets.

It roars and growls and is sinister and grave.

It has a tail which is burnt and brown. Anger pours out ton by ton, gallon by gallon.

It has eyes that flash red white and yellow, like a torch on a dark night.

It's a confused mess of grey rope, knotted and twisted, pulled and stretched.

There's an elephant's trunk hidden under the bonnet.

Katie Miles

Science can be learned as we write, and writing learned as we do science. Also, science is poetic in the broadest sense: the notion that there is a gulf fixed between science and art is a sentimental delusion fostered by philistines on both sides. Look at telescopic photographs of moments in the life of the universe, or microscopic ones of blood cells, and, if we aren't blind, we can see sources of poetry, narrative, painting and dance. We can also see art in the workings of an engine, and this should be an encouragement to those industrialists and politicians who worry, reasonably enough, about the education system's bias against the world of manufacturing.

If this sounds obvious, it isn't to the originators of the subject-based structure of the National Curriculum. Despite them, there are many ways of stimulating vivid writing that also lead to scientific learning. For example, car engines can enrich both scientific understanding and our experience as writers. 'I think that is for ...' a child will hypothesise, as she stares into the engine. It needs little imagination for us to consider how we might push the child further, to other investigations, on the strength of this roughly drafted hypothesis.

I can feel the sharp blades of the fan, the spark plugs all ready to ring out, the pistons ready to crash into action. The key turns and the engine shudders, the fan sprinting around, the battery firing the spark plugs. The pistons shudder power into the grating gearbox as fumes choke themselves out of the exhaust. The wide black air cooler is like a squashed tin, trying to cool the roary flamey dragony engine working itself into hysterics.

I can hear Mummy grating the gears like a lion roaring. Our engine is getting louder as it purrs past a smelly, fumy lorry. Now it's speeding over the road ahead.

My mum's car engine goes vroom vroom. The engine jogs and judders, the engine smells oily. It is quite a funny shape. When my mum starts the car it goes jugga jugga. On some places it is like rubbing your hand on a smooth piece of wood and other places are nobbly.

The engine is like a living baby struggling to move. It's running faster and faster, it's getting hotter and hotter, it's starting to crawl along the road . . . It's like a man puffing and panting along the road . . .

The engine is black and greasy. The engine is chugging happily to itself. The engine smells of oil and grease. The wheels of the engine are round with tyres that are blown up. The engine goes grrrrr when it starts and purrrrrs when it stops. When you put your finger on the rusty engine it's like a cheese grater.

(*Christian, 8*)

The engine on my dad's car is a square shape. The wires look like Spaghetti Junction. The engine struggles to start. It works like the inside of a mechanical robot strutting along. Fumes from the engine smell like being at a petrol station. The radiator at the front of the car is like a cattle grid and it also looks like an air vent. It coughs like someone who smokes when it starts and it pants like a dog.

If you break down it's the engine's fault.

It screeches like a bird when the breaks are put on.

(*Rebecca, 8*)

I collect bits and pieces of old engines, to give presence to this writing, and some close observational drawings frequently emerge quite naturally from this stimulus.

Other mechanical objects are useful for writing and drawings. A visit, for example, to the boiler house and the kitchens, if it can be arranged, is useful, or to a local building site. So are complicated kitchen implements. And when children go out of school, they should get into the habit of carrying notebooks or clipboards with them – not to answer questionnaires, but to record impressions, which they might find useful later, in words and sketches.

Crafted out of feeling

> After she went home the weather was horrid, and my Mum said 'Perhaps the sun liked Nanny'.

One of the problems teachers have with the National Curriculum – and even more with the booklets from the Schools Examinations and Assessment Council – is the contrast between a typical prose sentence grindingly assembled by a committee, and one crafted out of feeling, skill and love by an individual, like the one quoted above.

> Pupils should be taught how to handle, and be given an experience in using, a range of information texts in a variety of media. (Writers of 'Programmes of study for reading' that 'support attainment target 2' in 'English in the National Curriculum'.)

And then, in Pack C of the SEAC booklets, on page 5, we read 'It is important to know about the child's response to the individual tasks since these are the child's attainments.' Here a singular subject, 'response', has acquired a plural object, 'attainments'.

Grindingly assembled is the only phrase. Rhythmless ineptitudes like this make sure that Pack C goes largely unread, because most of us are used to reading clearer sentences – in novels, for example, and in letters from friends, and in newspapers. And the result is that SEAC and NCC papers have not received proper critical attention. It is simply too difficult a task – not intellectually, but in terms of stamina.

They've been the butt of jokes: Ted Wragg has seen them off, for example. But they are largely unread because they are largely unreadable. In contrast:

My Grandma is quite old now. I don't quite know because I've never asked. She lives at No. 25 _____ Rd., Edmonton. Her house is very old and she has a leak in the front room. Each side of the window in her front room is a portrait of herself and Grandad. I don't know if it's still there because we never go in there now. We only go in the back room which has an electric fire where the old fireplace is. She never uses the fireplace now. 'It's too much trouble' she says.

My grandad is dead now. He used to call me 'Little Boy' even though I'm a girl. He always used to say to me 'If you stop biting your nails, I'll give you ten shiny penny pieces'. This was before we changed to decimals.

In the Easter holidays my Grandma used to come and stay with us. She talked, now and then, about my Grandad and what he used to say and do. I could see that her eyes were watery.

After she went home the weather was horrid, and my Mum said 'Perhaps the sun liked Nanny'.

Eleven-year-old Jill wrote this piece in 1972. I came across it while looking through old files, and it moved me again after nearly two decades. This was, of course, because of the subject matter – the death of one grandparent and his family's reactions to it. But it was also because the treatment showed off an eye for detail, like those symmetrically placed portraits, the unused parlour and the little boy joke. The spareness helped, too: Jill builds up a catalogue of things that stand for her Grandad, and never once mentions her own emotions. And, as a result, her emotions come across the years clearer than a video.

But what moves me most is the pair of sentences 'If you stop biting your nails, I'll give you ten shiny penny pieces. This was before we changed to decimals.' These sentences provide the only evidence that the piece wasn't written last term: they are the only out-of-date words, and they remind me (as they are reminding you, if you're old enough, and if you're reading this at a relaxed moment) of those huge copper discs, that made your hand smell, twelve of which made a shilling.

The pennies, by being out-of-date, point up the timelessness of the writing. Hardy wrote that 'War's annals will cloud into night' before the story – the writing, the telling – of 'a maid and her wight' die. As various commentators have pointed out, the officials who censored Pushkin are forgotten while *Eugene Onegin* lives. And although Auden overstated the case when he said 'Time . . . Worships language and forgives/Everyone by whom it lives . . .', it was an exaggeration in the right direction.

Long after LMS, CDT, INSET, TVEI, GRIST, SEAC, and NCC have shrivelled like censors in a totalitarian state, there will be a child in a school writing: making notes on paper or on a screen, to try to understand her grandfather's death, or the arrival of a new baby brother, or the way a tree grows.

I had taught Jill, who wrote this piece, by getting conversations going in a top junior classroom about old people. Alec Clegg's book *The Excitement of Writing* (1965) had been the starting point for this lesson, as it was the starting point for so much vivid work in the late sixties and seventies. It quickly emerged that the children had observed their elderly relations and friends with great acuity: they talked about their skin, their hair, their way of walking, their front rooms, with affection and interest. Once they'd been told they had to record their impressions of the old people using words 'the other won't think of' they had little difficulty in working with power and empathy.

To be fair to the booklets in the National Curriculum, I concede that writing under extraordinary pressure for an audience that includes politicians and administrators as well as teachers was an impossible task. And there are some ringing, confident sentences in the English documents. Understandably, there are more in the sections on writing than there are elsewhere. Here's one, from English for ages 5 to 11:

> The best writing is vigorous, committed, honest and interesting . . .

The problem, though, is that this paragraph continues:

> . . . We have not included these qualities in our attainment targets because they cannot be mapped on to levels . . .

This is a serious warning: if we restrict our teaching to those things that can be so 'mapped', we will miss out all vigour, commitment, honesty and interest. And that should make our palms sweat with anxiety. After all, as the paragraph continues:

> . . . all good classroom practice will be geared to fostering these vital qualities.

The word 'vital', of course, means 'concerned with, or essential to, organic life'. The reverse is true: writing that is restricted to the bloodless advice of SATs, ATs, levels and Key Stages will be dead.

The most successful teachers of writing will continue to work beyond the National Curriculum, helping children to produce poems, stories, reportage and notes that will still be read with a kind of thrill twenty years after they were written. And it is the National Curriculum itself that spells out clearly why this is one of a teacher's most important tasks; whether the work produced has a purely aesthetic function or, as in my final examples, serves the teaching of religion and history.

Vashti had often proved inspired in her writing of myths (see her poem 'To the Sun' in my anthology Clock Work, from *This Way That Way* 1989). Here she works in the same field, but in prose:

One day God said 'I'm lonely. I will make something to keep me company'. He made a dog, but the dog looked sad. 'What's the matter?' Dog said, 'God, I'm so lonely'.

So God made lots of dogs, but they ate Him out of house and home, so He said 'I will make you a world and you can live on it'. So He did, but there was not any light, or food or water. So God got some fire and rolled it into a ball and threw it above the earth.

'I will call you Sun,' said God, feeling very pleased.

But then something very strange happened. Bits of the sun kept falling off. It did not seem to be very pleased to be a ball in the sky. God grabbed what was left of the sun and took it apart. He put some clay in the middle of it and put it back in its place and the little bits of the sun that had fallen off the sun He called stars.

Then He sat on the edge of His garden with His legs dangling down into space. He stamped on His world and made holes in it. He went into a well and got water and put it in all the little holes.

Just then God's friend Mountain came along, stamping and shaking salt all over the place. 'Don't do that!' said God. 'Now look what you have done!' Mountain looked at God's world. There were lumps in it and in the water was salt. God sat down and said 'Dear oh dear. I wish there were not vibrations. I don't see why you had to stamp, Mountain, and as for shaking salt, look what you have done to my sea!'

But the dogs guessed that this might happen, so they had made tunnels in the earth, and some of the fresh water had run into them. Then the dogs had found some un-dry clay and made a cover for them and called them river, stream, lake and spring.

Meanwhile God had decided to call the lumps mountains after His friend. The dogs said 'We want food' so God made some other kinds of creatures and things for them to eat, but they argued about their food, so God made a chart for everyone like this:

COW ⟶ GRASS

Then the dogs went up to God. 'We want something to see and sleep on' they said.

So God made plants, trees, shrubs, and grass. Then He went to bed.

The next day God got up. The dogs came round Him and pestered Him all morning for something to play with. In the end God got cross. 'Be satisfied' He said, so they went away from a very tired God.

He went straight to bed and the dogs made a plan. They got all of God's clay and got in a long line. One by one they solemnly got some clay, threw it into the sky and named it.

There was Mars, Saturn, and a lot of others. Then God woke up. He decided to make the dogs something to do. He got His bag with clay in it. There was only a little bit. God knew at once it was the dogs, so He made them two things to make them work as a punishment. He called them humans. Then he ran out of clay.

Well, at least it gave the dogs something to do, and God was satisfied.

(*Vashti*, 9)

'Gradually I came to know where I was' wrote Augustine. Through narrative about their lives, their fantasies, their religion, their experiences of science, children become writers, and come gradually to know where they are, and how to make their wants and provisional understandings known.

CHAPTER 3

Off the Wall and Out of the Frame

with Duncan Allan

The artist is not a special kind of man, but every man is a special kind of artist. (Ananda Coomaraswamy)

This is a case study of an art project in Tattingstone School, a small rural primary school in Suffolk. The head of this school, Duncan Allan, and his wife collect pictures and sculptures, mostly British work of the years between the wars. And the project is, in a sense, an extension of a personal passion. Indeed, all the art, drama, dance, poetry, narrative and music in this book can be seen in the same way.

But these arts are also rooted in educational values. The headteacher wanted to make his school a centre where art was valued as a way of learning, much as successive deans at Chichester Cathedral, which owns art by John Piper, Graham Sutherland and Marc Chagall, have used art to teach worshippers about God's relationship with humankind.

Subsequently, the headteacher commissioned a stained glass window for the school. High on an internal wall, Surinder and Roland Warboys' glass depicts great crested grebes from the nearby reservoir, bringing outside light into the classroom, which is filled with children's work: adult-sized puppets for the Christmas play, for example, and linocut prints, based on pictures by Van Gogh, Francis Bacon and others. Eleven-year-old Nancy sold me one of her linocuts based on Blake's Nebuchadnezzar for 50p. The children talk about art with an astonishing assurance. When I was last there, they'd just visited the Sainsbury Centre, the gallery at the University of East Anglia, and Christopher, aged nine, had been very taken with a triptych:

44

There's these three pictures by Francis Bacon. One, this person sitting down all swirly, and then he's on the floor all pink and writhing and in the third one his feet are all swirly. It's brilliant. It's all what you feel yourself ... No, they're not scary — but they're weird ...

Here is real art appreciation, the close examination that such work requires, a contrast with a teacher-dominated classroom where children are offered pale reproductions of Van Gogh, and asked to discuss them. Sam didn't like the Bacon: 'I couldn't get a shape out of it but I liked the statues by John Davies. I've done a picture like the Van Gogh man walking.' Aaron 'liked one where this bloke was falling over and this woman was crying'.

Duncan told me: 'We're talking about discovery, asking questions, exploration, solving problems, and that's a lot of National Curriculum science, maths, technology ... If we get back to what art is, well, the whole purpose of it is a means towards discovery. If you're not experimenting, it's not art for me, and experimenting is what art and science and everything have in common ... Art should be just as hard work as everything else. It's not minds in the morning, hands in the afternoon for us ... My classes are a lot less free than they used to be, partly because of the National Curriculum, partly because of my dual role as head and class teacher. To keep my sanity I can't feed off the children so much, I have to have things more structured.'

On the wall are a group of postcards of work from the Sainsbury Centre, including a Lucien Freud picture of a woman largely clothed, but with one breast exposed. Julia, aged seven said this was one of her favourites 'because of the dog in the background ... I don't like the lady, though, I don't like the look on her face'.

'We had a long chat about that picture and the nudes,' says Duncan. 'But we thought that, given our work in health education, sex education, it was daft, ridiculous, censoring pictures. So we didn't. And the children were great. When we suggested they work from pictures, some just took the dog out of that one, then later they looked at the whole thing, quite unselfconsciously.'

This openness spreads to everything. But the art especially is 'better than first year art school' said the TES photographer. Duncan feels isolated 'frankly, because of the level of work we achieve in art'.

'A place I've never been to', linocut 1992 by Dale Devereux Barker

Duncan gave me the following account of his work with an artist and a group of children. He'd been at the school only three months when these events took place. The school did not have a reputation for innovative work in the creative arts, and his impact on the school and the village may be imagined. He didn't, however, write up the project for nine months. Perhaps there is a certain orderliness, a tranquillity in the account that wouldn't have been there had it been more raw.

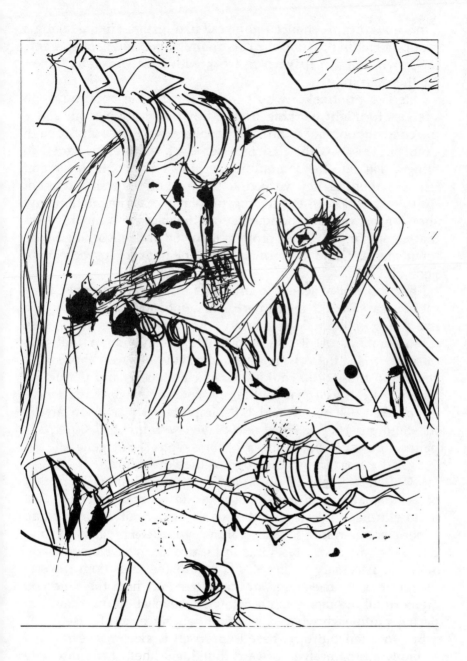

By an 11-year-old boy looking at Picasso's Woman with a Red Hat

(Duncan writes) A chance phone call had resulted in me taking a group of children, Anne the classroom helper and some parents to Crown Pools in Ipswich to work with Dale Devereux Barker for the morning.

Dale is a printmaker who had been given the opportunity to spend a fortnight working from a tiny observation room above the competition pool as artist in residence with Ipswich Borough Council. This was the first in a series of ventures designed to bring artists into the community and to allow people to see and talk with them as they worked; to bring art off the wall and out of the frame, to be seen as a creative process of experimentation; and showing, as with all experimentation, the messiness and mistakes that accompany it. Other projects involved artists working in the town's market, and at Portman Road, the home of Ipswich Town Football Club.

I had joined the school to find little in the way of exploratory art. To say what I mean here, I'd quote Raphael's idea of a line being a flight into eternity. Anyway, it was this sense of exploration, of discovery through art and in art that was missing. Also, there were sharp divisions between those who could and those who couldn't draw: inhibitions and prejudices within the children that could only have come from experiences in the past. There seemed little importance placed on art by the children. They dabbled and played with gimmicks; perhaps painted the odd shield for a history project. But generally art occupied a position on the edge of the curriculum.

So often we talk of an integrated curriculum or a project based/thematic approach – but what do we really mean? What it should mean is bringing the whole process of discovery and experimentation into the curriculum; of making judgements and decisions part of our teaching and learning: these elements are, after all, necessary to life itself, within the classroom, on the playground, on the street, in the home, and from the time you are born till the time you die. How effectively you use them will perhaps influence what satisfaction you get from life itself.

But so often a project-based approach is simply a term used to imply a progressive, forward thinking school. 'Let's integrate the curriculum' we say, and what do we do? We choose a topic: autumn, or minibeasts. If we're really thinking, we give it a classier title: Circles, Forces and Stress, Change; and then we sit around giving the children exercises based around the theme:

Collect some leaves, Write a poem about squirrels, Count conkers. I'm being cynical and over-simplifying; belittling thought processes – but when doing this are we really considering the educational value within the activities the children are doing? There may be some relevance in making cardboard shields to decorate a classroom and make it feel like a baronial hall but if this is the sole place of art then it is not good enough. An art curriculum that concentrates on this kind of decorative function is selling the children short. Can we honestly say that the children are experimenting or have been stretched emotionally or imaginatively?

Looking at the literature on Dale's proposed residency it seemed a good opportunity to start moving art into a more valued position within the curriculum. Dale appeared to be an artist who was approachable and humorous. The subject and setting seemed stimulating. I wanted to put the children in a position where they would be forced to work quickly and freely; where they would be unable to let their inhibitions take over. If the mind is continually being checked by thoughts of 'I can't do this' it becomes impossible to explore constructively. It seemed to me that being within the swimming baths with the noise and movement all around the children could not but be stimulated.

I had not met or even spoken to Dale before the visit but I had been able to get messages to him conveying broad ideas of loosening the children's approach to painting and drawing. Generally the children in school worked very tightly from their wrists, ignoring the overall flow of form and line but rather concentrating, millimetre by millimetre, on reproducing exact copies. I hoped we could begin to break away from this and at the same time show the parents the sort of experiences I was hoping to give the children in the future.

Looking through the brochure produced to advertise Dale's residency I felt encouraged by his experience and his comments. He had trained at the Slade School of Art, by custom a place of innovative work. Dale had travelled to California and Cyprus, places of colour and light, and I was certainly looking for an artist who would work with strong colour. His work also showed great simplicity of line. I didn't want work that would mystify or confuse the children. This is not to say that I would always wish to avoid such work but that this was not the right time. I needed someone whose work would be challenging but approachable and appealing.

Dale's introduction in the brochure was also helpful. He wrote of having the opportunity to work away from 'the often forboding (*sic*) art gallery' and of his aims of working in a 'visually exciting way'.

I was encouraged, too, by conversations with Rebecca Weaver, the Exhibition Organiser. She was excited by the possibility of introducing young children to Dale and, although he had never worked with children before, Dale (Rebecca said) seemed enthusiastic.

I find entering a swimming bath a strange experience. Immediately one becomes anonymous. There is that mixture of dampness, chlorine and warmth, and the sterile hospital feel of echoes, tiles and cleanliness; lines of hurried children with wet straggly hair and red swollen eyes; the straight lines and primary colours of modern architecture; and bare walls.

Standing amongst all this with the anticipation of waiting for a real artist to appear, what were we expecting? The children were quiet, excited, but nervous. A real artist, what were they expected to do? They couldn't draw or paint. What was he going to ask them? How could they match his skills? Dale appeared, with round spectacles and long hair parted down the centre, through which he continually ran his fingers. He was nervous, more nervous than the children, and spoke in a soft whisper. I found myself shaking an almost trembling hand. I warmed to him in a moment. Most headteachers like meeting nervous people: they let us show off our skill for putting them at their ease.

Dale led us upstairs to his studio and began to talk about his pictures, showing the children his lino cuts, the tools and his prints. Once amongst his work he appeared more relaxed and as the children began to respond with enthusiasm his nerves seemed to go. The children began to feel easier, more confident. Their fears were unfounded. Here was a person of wonderful sincerity who was reflecting the calmness and gentleness within his pictures. He respected them and was interested in who they were.

We hadn't got long. Eastern Counties Buses only run sporadically to the village and we couldn't afford the luxury of a hired coach. I had a few minutes to talk to Dale about what I was hoping for. Dale explained what he was hoping to do. The morning was to be split into two parts. Firstly the children were going to sit in the spectators' gallery with sheets of A4 paper and produce very quick sketches – snapshots – of what they saw. This was not to be a complete image of the pool but images of the swimmers. The children were going to be encouraged to look at the way water distorts an image. To look at what could be seen above and below the water, and how water magnifies and blurs.

The second part of the morning would be spent on large sheets of paper using the sketches as working drawings to produce murals with paint, crayon, pastel, and felt tip. This also set up the interesting position where the children, having worked individually, then had to come together and work as a group.

Dale spoke quietly to the children, showing them some of his pictures to illustrate his points, and it was good to see him growing in confidence with the positive responses of the children and their obvious delight at his work. His talk wasn't long but all the children went off knowing exactly what they were to do. Pencils, biros and felt tips were all ready and within a few minutes everyone was working. It was here that Dale really came alive, and once the children were working the parents began to take a more active part.

He began moving around the children, taking their work away as they were drawing. He spoke kindly and enthusiastically: 'That's great. Do another.' 'That's enough on that one. Now look at something else.' A child would look up from her work for a moment only to look down again to find a blank piece of paper and Dale moving off to someone else.

It was an inspired way of loosening the children. He was insisting that they work quickly; that their sketches were not precious images to be laboured over. Someone had drawn a head. 'That's enough, take it away!' There was an image of someone dangling their feet in the water. 'Save it and use it later.' He was getting them to look at as many shapes and effects as possible and not to concentrate on one thing. This may sound like a disorderly mess with little control or concentration but it was rather like being asked to run several 100 metre sprints one after the other, each one requiring maximum effort.

At the end of this I was skulking off to the coffee machine with the idea that this would be a managerial move: the boss being seen to do the menial tasks as well as the important ones, or that a happy staff well watered will work better. Basically, I was thirsty. Dale, Anne and the rest were busy sticking together huge pieces of paper.

Talking to Dale during the session was interesting. We so often confuse schooling with education. As teachers we are there to educate, or so we say. Usually though we are there to *school*, to teach skills, a one-way process of delivery which leaves us assessing children on a skills-based level. 'Are they able to do this? How well have I taught them to use a pencil?'

Dale is not a teacher by profession yet his approach has much to be envied. His view of the morning was as a two-way process, that education is a two-way process. He said to me that the response of the children was something new to him. It was a response that had helped him with his confidence and resolve.

Dale's brief was to produce a set of large murals for the walls of Crown Pools: work which was relevant to the pool, that is, paintings of swimmers. The murals would be hung on the huge blank walls to bring the place alive. Yet when he had finished these pieces, huge, bold, colourful and very funny works, he couldn't find anyone interested enough to help him put them up. No gallery staff with an interest in profit motive. No pool attendants or managers who thought it worthwhile.

The very weekend he was finishing his residency a competition was being filmed in the main pool. He was required to clear out of his makeshift studio to make way for the commentary team. And why had no-one the time to help him put up his huge hangings? Because they were all too busy installing and arranging the plants to make the place look nice for the TV cameras. Such is the place of art.

Similarly much of Dale's work is being bought up to grace the walls of new offices in Dockland. He is under no illusion here. Yes, it brings in the money, but he might as well be producing wallpaper. Small wonder, then, that a positive response from the children should put new confidence and resolve into him. They looked at his work and loved it for its colour, its humour, and its simplicity, and they were inspired by it.

Dale's art isn't intended to mystify. It is intended to be accessible. Something which all can enjoy; yet no-one seems to look. No-one except a group of children, parents and teachers who have had the joy of creating something with him. Who have laid down on the floor and watched him paint a swimmer spluttering for air and been asked to finish it off. To have joined in with a riot of colour and brushstrokes to illustrate the splash and noise of a dive; or simply to have been left alone because they are totally immersed in concentration which mustn't be broken. Parents who admitted they hadn't taken up a paintbrush since they left school worked with the children and loved every minute.

We talk of introducing children to different media and we so often treat it as some kind of sacred performance. 'Today, children, we are going to explore the medium of pastel.' Not at Crown Pools. Spread out were paints, crayons, pastels, felt tips. All there to experiment with. It is the initial teacher talk that is important. 'See how the runny paint looks like water. What happens when we put the paint over the pastel? Look at the colours when that man dives into the water. Look at the colour in the splashes. What can you see? At the time what can you see? Look at the shapes. See how the water bends the shapes.'

All the time Dale is asking the children to observe and interpret what is seen. Isn't that what we should be asking of poetry or drama or art or science or maths? I can see something happening. Can I untangle what is seen and interpret it? Can I record it in a way which gives an impression of how I felt when I saw it and how the person felt when they were doing it?

And the skills are there. The children are developing their skills in form and line. They are experimenting and questioning and making decisions. They have control, and are sharpening their powers of control over their materials, and their enthusiasm drives them on.

There were some lovely moments during the morning: times to just stand and watch. Those moments that we say we never have time for within the classroom. Times of assessment but really times to enjoy what is going on. For example – a brother and sister are working together on one large piece of paper but working on two totally separate drawings. The older child, the sister, has total dominance in terms of space. She has the centre of the paper and is producing a large drawing of a girl (herself?) in a bathing hat floating in the water with a large grin on her face. The brother has been relegated to the bottom right hand corner and is being forced to work on a very small scale.

Another older lad who doesn't read and who covers his inabilities with an aggressive image is lost in his work. He thinks he can't draw. His friends can, they can do everything well, or so he thinks, and they let him think it. I'd left most of them in school for that reason. He had found himself a corner and a large sheet of paper, perhaps a metre square, and was producing a picture which almost made one cry with pleasure. Two feet are sticking out of the water, all that remained visible of a diving swimmer, and around the image the splashes and ripples of the impact. The sound of the dive echoed out of the paper.

Dale was impressed and told Wesley so but had the sensitivity to stop him only for a moment. Wesley was working and didn't need disturbing. Extra praise would come later. I asked myself at the time, how many of us professionals would have had that sensitivity? How many of us, conversely, would have barged in with well-meaning shouts of encouragement, only to break the spell? Wesley went on holiday some months later to the Norfolk Broads and took a sketchbook with him.

In another corner, four older girls had set themselves up and were planning very carefully the layout and composition of their picture. This was in stark contrast to the group of younger boys next to them. For them, the only evident planning was that the paper was to represent the pool. On to, or into, this was being put a complete jumble of swimmers. There was no thought of which way up the paper went. This didn't bother them. Each boy was working on his own piece with no consideration of its relationship to the rest of the picture. What they were doing was experimenting with the effects of the paint on the paper: the differences between thin and thick paint and how it reacted when put over crayon, pastel, or felt tip.

As the group progressed they began to look for other spaces to fill and began to consider the work of others in the group and notice too the topsy-turvy nature of the layout. This seemed to bother some of the group more than the others, and they immediately began blaming others for their errors.

The group of girls continued with their planning. Three parents had moved towards them and spent the rest of the session working with them. This piece was the most mature of the morning. It was balanced and well-proportioned. The figures were full of life and action, made up of beautiful, economic brushstrokes. The whole thing was very controlled in technique and composition. Was anticipation of this success the reason why the parents felt safest working with this group?

In many ways these two groups had been working along the same lines. Both groups had been experimenting with different media and had been looking at line and form. They had also worked very freely without any apparent inhibition. They had met problems and overcome them, even if this meant, in some cases, blaming others. They'd found techniques which worked effectively and they'd incorporated these within their work, perhaps using them again later in the session.

Looking at the finished work from these two groups, I think it would be incorrect to say one was better than the other. What it did show was the maturity of the older group against the younger one, and perhaps the differences between boys and girls.

Walking back to the bus, Anne (the ancillary helper) and I decided to say nothing to the children about the morning. My mind goes back to teaching practice and advice in tutorials: talk of follow-up sessions and how to enlarge on your theme. Neither of us felt it necessary. Indeed, how could we follow it up? For us it had been totally exhilarating. To try and add to it at that time would have been pointless. In time we would work on the ideas and build upon what we had seen and learned.

It had been a morning of education for us and, we felt sure, for the children. All that was needed was time to enjoy; just as we enjoy the calmness of sitting in a car after a morning on a shingle beach during a storm. Would we try to follow that up? Would we force discussion about how we felt about what we'd seen? 'Let's make a list of words about the feelings we felt as we painted. And watch the spelling.' I've done it! Did it last week and got some good words but are there not times when we overdo it? And now we watch the spelling because AT (whatever) Level (whatever) tells us we must and so it becomes justifiable and easy. We no longer have to question our motives for doing it because it is law. As a teacher said to me recently 'If they want to me to tick off boxes let's go and get it out in the open. Tell me what I've got to do and I'll do it and then tick it off. Done. Simple as that'.

Often we imagine or assume we have done a good job. We ask the children 'Did you enjoy that?' 'Yes' they say. Would they dare say anything else? Nine months after the visit to Crown

Pools I asked the children involved what they remembered of the morning:

KELLY If you can't draw a person he'd ask you to look more carefully at the person and feelings would come up inside of you and make your hands want to draw.

CATHERINE Once you saw how easy it was you just didn't want to stop drawing.

NANCY There was one of people diving off a board. He seemed to do lots of simple pictures.

KELLY When you saw his pictures you said 'Oh no' but when he showed you it seemed easy and your hand went all loose. He was a very understanding kind of person. He'd help you and make suggestions.

ESME His pictures seemed to be done slowly with one line and not lots of lines. The shapes were just one line.

CATHERINE When he dipped his paintbrush in the paint he just carried on until the brush ran out of paint so as you got one flowing line.

A letter came from Duncan Allan a month later:

'I have tried Dale's suggestion of increasing the length of the paintbrush handle and your suggestion of perhaps using a ruler rather than a long cane. I have initially used just black paint and concentrated on producing line. The results have been very good. The children's control over the brush is very fine and the lines flow beautifully. The composition of the pictures has also been very good and in some respects this is the most exciting part. So often children's paintings seem to concentrate on a central subject with the rest of the picture filled in for the sake of filling in: large areas of paint which have little bearing on the picture itself. The end result often seems to belittle what was intended, a tiny subject surrounded by a mass of blue sky or green grass. The reason for this does I think result from this problem of attempting to use a paintbrush like a pencil and working in very tight movements from the wrist, forgetting the overall proportion of the paper. By extending the length of the brush and thus magnifying the wrist movement the initial subject of the painting immediately assumes bigger proportions and the panic situation of 'Oh hell, I've got all this paper to fill' is immediately removed and the children seem happier to work more constructively. I'm looking forward to the summer when we can get outside and work on a really big scale.'

So often, as Duncan suggests, art is used merely as a decorative aid for history teaching. Other areas of the National Curriculum will also, no doubt, use art as a hook to hang things on: 'We do a lot of art here' said one head to me 'because the children get so much language out of it.' We can make our learning in language more fun by doing a lot of art around it. We can lighten the tedium of making large sums of money by hanging a Dale Devereux Barker picture in our Docklands office.

But there should be an integration. John Lancaster in his book *Art in The Primary School* (1990) has neatly designed suggestions for working with music, mathematics, science, history, geography and art across the curriculum – using, for example, the theme 'Water'. Knowledge is not divided into ten subjects. Such a grid patterning is only for organisational convenience. The integration is there anyway without our forcing it. As the children watched Dale working, or worked themselves, having listened to him talk, and watched the swimmers and their effect on the water, they were not just learning about art. They were learning about water. They were, for example, making informal hypotheses: When she hits the water, the water will . . . They were 'observing familiar materials and events in their immediate environment, at first hand, using their senses'. They were talking to each other, negotiating meanings and exploring words. They were thinking. They were, to use the NCC's now commonplace phrase, 'speaking and listening'.

Painting shields in history may be cross-curricular, but, as Rob Barnes asks in an unpublished paper, is it art? As he says, 'There is nothing quite like the excitement of understanding one subject by encountering it through another' – but he goes on to point out the dangers of this approach, most memorably with this story:

> . . . a group of children are given the job of painting large paper trees for drama in the school hall. The design of the paper shapes is conditioned in advance by the drama itself and the children have perhaps two shades of green each. They are left to their own devices to fulfil a predetermined design. The result of this strategy is to *make use of children as slaves* [author's italics] to the arts project.

Or a child has written a poem. 'Now draw a picture about it.' What is this kind of work? Why do we do it? It has no serious relationship to art because it has no exploratory function. This kind of work belittles not only art, but the reality of life in previous times with its sentimentalisation, its averting of the eyes from the realities of life as lived by nearly all the people. A Viking shield in bright poster paint takes the place of the violence and hunger that we are frightened of. A profile of Anne Boleyn done from yet another brass allows us to ignore the power politics that dehumanised king, woman and courtier alike. And if this is to bring politics, feminism and social class into education – why weren't they there anyway?

Enough, then, of Viking shields, painting scenery and doing a drawing after your writing. This notion of art as decoration, as something to take our minds off the distressing or boring realities of our lives, is common. This is a writer of fantasy stories talking on *Woman's Hour* in 1989: 'These stories are successful because people want to get away from their boring little lives ... most people's lives are so banal and our stories excite them.' This seems to be the rationale behind the decorative view of art. It has its place in a certain view of classrooms, too, when writers – John Lancaster for example – talk about the 'aesthetically pleasing'. This view of art dominated certain educational authorities in the sixties and seventies.

Schools, to judge by appearances, might have been built of natural hessian, and displays of Victorian machinery, stuffed animals and teazles threatened the safety of any child breaking the school's first rule by running along a corridor. This view of aesthetic education is still legitimated by some of HMI and LEA advisers, who encourage teachers to spend hours arranging displays and helping children to bind their own books.

Duncan believes that 'the richness of a child's environment and the aesthetic nature of one's classroom or school is a great part of this. Call it an ambience or whatever you like but it's present in one's house, in art galleries, and it can influence feelings and atmosphere. The seventies Habitat schools of plants and hessian are just fashion and have changed but the underlying reasons are still valid'.

But 'pleasantness' is simply not a strong enough concept for anything concerned with the arts and education. It is related to the way we can avert our eyes from the inner-city realities by hanging a picture of poppies in the corn outside Kersey, or fishing boats drawn up on the sand at Aldeburgh. Often, the lowest form of art in schools is merely there to fill time: bright ideas to get the teacher off the hook while he or she does something really important, like assessment, or phonics with the less able.

Duncan Allan identifies a distinction between schooling and education. 'Creativity cannot be delivered like the daily pinta.' 'The purpose of education,' Stenhouse wrote 'is to make us freer and more creative.' 'That' says Allan 'means we must have more time to experiment, to play. In industry this would be called research, but the government are cutting back on that in our universities ... The purpose of schooling is to fit us for society as society sees itself.'

Art is conventionally placed, like a Grecian Urn, on a pedestal; or inside a frame, often behind a bullet-proof glass. Even in Duncan Allan's account, the artist has the equivalent of a garret, a tiny room placed above the real life of the swimming pool. And he has to move out with his chattels quickly when the stars of our age turn up, the TV cameras and the sports commentators.

Art is forbidding if it tries to stretch beyond the merely pleasant. Sport is inviting. Notwithstanding Dale, art usually mystifies, is not accessible. 'Most people ignore most poetry' Adrian Mitchell has famously said 'because most poetry ignores most people.' Even though Dale's work didn't ignore people, and was, indeed, accessible, most people still ignored it. As far as the staff at the pool were concerned, or the wealthy businessmen in Docklands who bought Dale's pictures, whatever those pictures were like, they brought with them the traditional baggage of art and were nothing essentially to do with them and their lives – except as wallpaper.

We talk to children about a new medium, as Duncan Allan says, as if it were something 'sacred'. Sport is open. Art worries, is displaced by pot plants. Something has got between people and art that wasn't there when the cave dwellers communicated with each other by drawing, or when someone sang about Lord Thomas and Fair Eleanor, or when hoi polloi piled into the pit at the Globe theatre. Art has lost – even deliberately cut off – its relations with most people.

That is one way of looking at this problem. But art deliberately defamiliarises for other reasons. That is why novels are written in experimental forms; indeed, all novels are experimental, because no novel truly enacts the passage of time it describes. That is why painting goes through passages when the experimentation seems extreme: because the previous experiments have become stale and emotionally unprofitable. They have brought artists to a point where the observer can say 'This is an artist who understands and has full control over his or her medium ...' and no more. This is the point where decadence sets in.

Art must defamiliarise in order to survive. As long as the *Daily Mail* art critic is happy with what the Tate Gallery is displaying, artists are failing. They have to remake the familiar in unfamiliar ways. If art distresses people, then it is doing its job, which, above all, is to be noticeable and the opposite of dull ... It needs, too, as Barthes says (see introduction), a familiarity with the past even if this familiarity is used to criticise. Mostly this knowledge will be useful in building a new aesthetic, another way of understanding what it is to be an artist, a critic, an understander, an explorer of art.

Dale gets the children to use working drawings. They would be called drafts in the field of writing. It is in the draft stage that the most powerful learning takes place. In his 1976 book *An Introduction to Curriculum Research and Development* Lawrence Stenhouse describes a process model for designing and evaluating curricula. He quotes criteria for evaluating what is happening in a classroom that are concerned with engagement, collaboration, activeness, redrafting, inquiry – in other words, all qualities that are to do with process, rather than with a means-end model.

Too much work in the visual arts in schools has been concerned also with a means-end model, where the teacher is constantly aiming at what will happen next: the finished picture, eventually mounted three times and displayed on parents' evening. The wittiest and most stylish rebuttal of the constant use of targets and putative ends in education comes from Normon Nicholson, in his poem 'Rising Five' (see *Modern Poetry*, edited by John Rowe Townsend, OUP 1971) where that ubiquitous school phrase is transformed gradually through 'rising June', 'rising night', 'rising soon' – to 'rising dead'. A process allows us to concentrate on the value of an experience here and now. Targets, for all their legitimisation in the National Curriculum, concentrate on the future.

If Nicholson is stylish, Stenhouse is exhaustive and damning: 'Education as induction into knowledge is successful to the extent that it makes the behavioural outcomes of the students unpredictable.' It is in the unpredictability of the work the children did with Dale Devereux Barker that the education lies;

not in what can be mapped out in targets for reasons of what Stenhouse calls 'socially approved goals'.

Duncan's pleasure (almost 'crying with pleasure') is evident throughout this account: in the artist's work in his teaching, in the children's work. He is almost sensual, hedonistic. He is non-puritanical. He is happy to play. One aspect of Duncan's play when he is not being a teacher is in his and his wife's collecting of pictures. When you go to their house you are conscious of art everywhere. They collect work mostly by British painters between the wars, and two of their favourites are Cedric Morris and Arthur Lett Haines. They spend time at a dealer's house, and when they can't afford something they lust after, they borrow it on indefinite loan.

When they have bought a new piece, Duncan characteristically says to you, before you've got your coat off or even been offered a drink, 'Look at that line, that is beautiful, look at the way it sweeps around . . .' Eventually he runs out of words, because they are notoriously inadequate when we talk about art or pleasure; so he pours wine or tea, looking at his new picture. The main feature of the room on the left of the entrance is a large oil by Piero San Salvadore of a rather fierce old woman looking through a door frame that somehow becomes part of the picture frame. There is a ballet dancer by Adrian Ryan on an adjacent wall, and everywhere there are drawings. When the Allans went to Greece two years ago, they brought back through the customs a neolithic copy of an idol from prehistoric Crete that weighs over 45 pounds.

I am labouring this because Duncan is not just a teacher, but a man who collects pictures, listens to blues and jazz music, walks on shingle beaches in storms. What do they of education know who only education know? Perhaps the first prerequisite of any teacher is that she or he should be passionate about something other than education, and not ashamed of bringing that passion into the classroom. As Duncan said to me, 'The best moments are when you're simply relating to the children as human beings, you're not thinking of teaching them anything.'

When he is looking at and buying pictures, Duncan is playing: engaging in an activity because he wants to. In a nursery recently, a four-year-old, looking at a pile of old cans, sticks and other rubbish, said to the teacher, 'I want to make a climbing frame for spiders'. In the subsequent play, he learned about several things:

what structures will support others, for example. Similarly, Duncan learns as he plays: about art, about his own nature, as he reflects on a new picture or on a picture he might buy, or would buy if he could afford it.

Play is a recognition that we are human beings first. That our learning is not only what we gain through schooling, but what our everyday play activities lead us towards. 'Writing' says Irwin Shaw 'is finally play' (*Writers at Work*, 5th series, 1981). Duncan is conscious that he and the other adults in the setting are being educated too – as they play.

HMI always talk about following up. One said to me in an art gallery in Ipswich, where a class of children from my school were examining some African art, and imitating it: 'I admire the confidence with which the children look at these pictures, and the way they use their pencils ... their concentration is admirable ... I wish I could find the time to see how you are going to follow this up ... What are you thinking of doing?' (quoted in *Here Comes the Assembly Man*, Falmer 1989).

Duncan scorns it. It seems to be rooted in a puritanism that knows humankind was born in sin, conceived in iniquity; that as sexual pleasure is therefore sinful, so by extension any pleasure is; that therefore all activities must have a point, that all activities must be fully milked for their educational value. Among the necessary conditions for the making of art is a freedom, some moments of licence from schooling constraints. The most powerful of those constraints is the follow-up, with its time and motion insistence, with its language about cost-effectiveness.

Play is arguably the key notion here. When the artist waits for inspiration, she plays – whether with lines and form, or words, or notes. Sometimes this play is doodling, sometimes strumming. It can be making lists, or writing a paragraph about your grandfather and changing the word 'grandfather' to 'coriander' or 'jurisprudence' throughout. A time and motion man would cut all this activity out, not understanding its vital part in getting art started.

Children understand play, though. The National Curriculum has problems with it, being more concerned with schooling than education. When it tells us that (AT4 Science, Level 3) 'Pupils should know that some life forms became extinct a long time ago and others more recently', it is tempting us as teachers to a cynical form of schooling that will imply 'I've told you that, now you know it'. It will veer away from any kind of hedonistic play, any kind of pleasure in the search for understanding of evolution.

And then, over a year after Duncan's first meeting with Dale, Duncan said to me, 'Could I have a copy of what we've written so far about Dale? I want to put in an application for a residency at Tattingstone.'

CHAPTER 4

And in the Market Place

with Duncan Allan

'I've got to tell someone and I thought of you ... We got the residency!'

That was Duncan on the phone the following term. Simply to have an artist in residence in a school in days when money is tight and the priorities are all on science, technology and management isn't just a joy for the school concerned with art: it's also a political act of impudent proportions. This was taking place, after all, in days when *The Independent* reported:

> John MacGregor, the Secretary of State for Education and Science, suggested at the Professional Association of Teachers' conference that art, music and physical education – which includes dance, should no longer be compulsory for 14 to 16-year-old pupils in the National Curriculum ... In a letter to Mr MacGregor, Anthony Everitt, Secretary General of the Arts Council, describes the measure as 'very worrying'.
>
> He wrote: 'Arts subjects already appear to have been marginalised. Discussion of them has been delayed and they have been put to the bottom of the list of priorities for the National Curriculum working groups ... and already arts subjects are under threat ...' (6 August 1990)

There are two ways of looking at this marginalisation, from an arts-biased point of view. One is the line taken by Mr Everitt: the arts are considered unimportant, and this is a disgrace. But is there any chance that Duncan Allan, given the total exclusion of the arts from the National Curriculum, will stop teaching them? He will go on, as you and I will, offering children paint, pencils, clay and other media regardless of what comes down on to him from above. He will go on buying books of poems, and reading from them to the children. His colleagues will continue the dance tradition the school is slowly building up, and will buy more musical instruments. This will be in spite of advisers/inspectors roaming schools with checklists to see if children are 'on task'.

Indeed, in arts-committed schools the marginalisation might be good news, because suppression can bring out the strengths in teachers, much as poetry thrives in totalitarian regimes. The risk is in schools where the arts have never really had a serious presence: where they can now say with the support of their elders and betters, Secretaries of State, advisers, inspectors: Back to the basics. Forget the flummery of art.

We can see more clearly the political nature of any stance on the arts when we note that the managerialism of the last fifteen years has been the yardstick against which (as David Constantine has put it) we have defined our teaching of the arts. He says that the values of recent years have been purely 'mercantile', but the market leads inevitably to *The Sun* and the dreariest Australian soap. Teaching the arts makes the teacher believe, as a first step, that human beings are capable of better than that, of honesty and imagination, of being makers of things. To use a managerialistic phrase, if we 'raise standards' we will do it by rejecting the managerialism that only has place for the tamest art on its walls and in its CD players.

I had already used an artist in residence at my last school, and the following extracts from my book *Here Comes The Assembly Man* will give a flavour of the nine days:

> Emmanuel Taiwo Jegede gives the children a piece of clay each and tells them to make an egg. I watch them roll the clay around in their hands, greatly enjoying the experience, giggling and relishing the sheer feel of the stuff. Then they put the eggs in a little pile: each child gets a glimpse of his or hers, and then, blindfold, they have to tell if the egg they're offered is their own.
>
> I notice Emmanuel's faith: in his art, in his techniques, in the children. They are strangers to him but he trusts them: with his teaching, and with a beautiful ceramic bowl which his catalogue prices at £850.
>
> Later in groups of three the children carve a polystyrene cube, 12 x 12 inches, using knives borrowed from the kitchen and spokeshaves bought for the purpose. He asks them to choose a shape they fancy: a table with something on it – fruit, flowers, for

example; or a man reading. Polystyrene crumbs are everywhere, like leprosy, or snow.

He tended to make life easier with a phrase that sounded sentimental when I first heard it, but which later came to re-assure me: 'Emmanuel, could you spend some time with the nursery?' 'No problem.' 'Can we put on an exhibition in the Burns Elliot Hall' (in the town centre) 'with your work and some of the kids?' 'No problem.' 'We're putting you up for two nights with one of the teachers.' 'No problem.'

For the three weeks he was involved with Cowper School, he lent us some of his work: eight framed drawings, a bronze, an unfinished plaster cast; and copies of his catalogue, which contained translations of his poems. He also left with us some Nigerian and Ghanaian textiles. I loved the drawings especially, their powerful Yoruba faces, hands, eyes; and their dynamic construction.

The issue of residencies throws up interesting questions. The artist brings to the setting a different bag of expectations from the institution. This is not to descend into some post-romantic, sentimental image of the artist as the human being unfettered by society's claims. One poet I know claims that great men (*sic*) – and here he lists Churchill and Pasternak – need more of things than other men: more food, more drink and, of course, more love and more sex. They also need total freedom in any setting to express themselves. This extreme Dyonisiac view of the artist is valueless and harmful because the artist is also a citizen.

Any school is part of society, and as such has some duty to induct children into that structure. If it has (as I would claim) a duty to make children critically aware of that society, it does not require the sentimental fallacy I've described above. An artist in residence is likely to throw into relief the dilemmas built into this crux.

What follows is an account of the residency of Dale Devereux Barker at Tattingstone. While for Duncan Allan it was an experience to be seen on its own, for me it was part of a tradition that had begun with Emmanuel Jegede.

Four-year-old James sits on the floor at Tesco looking at several hundred bananas. Tongue out, mouth wide, he works with a big black felt tip pen. Every sweeping curve forms the edge of a banana. Six quick strokes gives three bananas joined at the

By a six-year-old girl looking at an Emmanuel Jegede painting

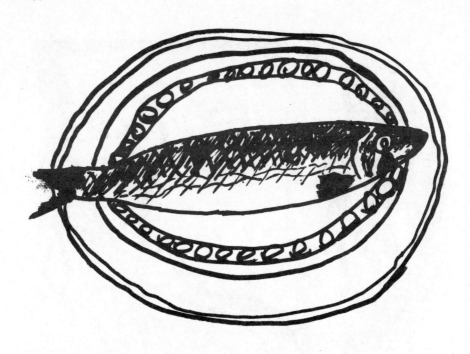

A nine-year-old's drawing of a fish in a supermarket

top. Then big open strokes in circles produce a set of oranges.

We almost wrote the word 'play' in that second sentence – and there is certainly a playfulness about both Dale Devereux Barker's methods and results, just as there is about James. Dale constantly experiments with pieces of card, often cut to the bottle shape which has been one of his recurrent symbols over the past three years. 'Collage,' he says 'is an important and useful way of working, because it mirrors the way we make sense of the world, adding together and layering information to fathom things out.'

In fact, there is much in common between the method of these four-year-olds, who started school a week ago and who are now working in Tesco, and that of Dale, who says 'I wouldn't go into the studio everyday (i) unless I enjoyed it and (ii) if I knew exactly what my pictures were going to end up looking like.' He constantly emphasises two elements in work: pleasure and experimentation. The children are enjoying themselves and wondering what will happen. You can tell both from their eyes, which are expectant, engaged: unlike those occasions when their

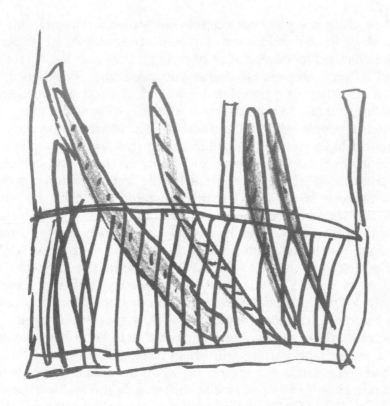

A seven-year old girl draws a trolley in the supermarket.

task is merely to catch information tossed to them in a lecture.

This is art off the pedestal, out of the frame, and literally in the market place. Literally, because the subject matter Dale has chosen for his residency at Tattingstone School is the supermarket: 'I encourage the children to look more closely at familiar surroundings. We went looking for art and we found it ... like Jean Dubuffet says "True art always crops up whenever you don't expect it".

'It's not about photographic representation, it's a starting point where children's imagination gets fired. I'll attempt to guide and fuel their skills and imagination, and the supermarket is a good place to try it, at least partly because we don't usually associate it with art.

'Yes, there is a place for careful observational drawing, but at this stage in the child's development art is mainly for experimentation, exploration, a way of trying things out, seeing them from different angles. Of course you need some experience of technique, there is a time for disciplined, difficult observational drawing, but taught with the understanding of how and why ... there are people who are fanatical in their attempts to produce a perfect likeness ... The children, though, are happy playing with abstract shapes, looking for balance in shape and colour.'

Tattingstone School is the venue for the first exhibition of some new Barker oils. Gallery 1 is the classroom – scruffy, because only last week the builders were here, and there was plaster all over the place. The school house, which is usually a set of small teaching rooms, is quieter and more orderly. In contrast, Dale has exhibited at the ICA, the Royal Academy, the Barbican, as well as in the USA. His most recent work is influenced by a stay in Western Australia. He wouldn't sell one of us two new oils based on this recent experience: 'They are the best ones ... Always I've sold prints, and I've been able to keep one ... Oils are a one-off and parting with them has become very hard.'

These oils snatch at that moment when the aircraft door opens on a new country and you smell a different air and see new colour schemes. Dale said 'If you asked me to paint a landscape in this country I couldn't do it, it's too familiar ... the problem is you know the feel of the dirt too well.'

Later he wrote to me, in notes commenting on an early draft of this chapter: 'About learning, knowledge, ability, freedom, all that stuff – I don't want to discuss it, I just want to add to it.' In Tesco he crouches, concerned not to make early judgements. When he stands up again, twice as tall as many of the children, and runs his fingers through his long fair hair he encourages them in a quiet voice. Later, he comments:

'I do worry about imposing my values ... As soon as we start holding children's pictures up we're saying publicly what is good, we're putting a filter on what's good and what's bad ... trimming and mounting children's work, it's mass editing ... We don't like all that white paper, let's cut it off. That's terrible, like listening to a symphony and saying, I like that bit, cut out the rest. But the children know exactly where they want things to go. The white space around is important.'

Dale begins to see the child/teacher/artist relationship from a new perspective. He asks eight-year-old Christabel to wash her hands. 'No, I want to keep them dirty. It shows I'm a real artist.' At the end of each day, he is very tired, and ready to question the value of his contribution: 'I often feel I'm trying to show them how good their drawings are, but they already know that ... The identity crisis is complete − an artist trying to free his own work showing a group of children the freedom of their own drawings − absurd! ... Who is teaching who? Picasso said he could draw like Raphael at 14, but it took him another fifty years before he could draw like a child.'

The children, with a team of adults, visited Tesco on the first day of the residency to gather data for the fortnight. The supermarket was welcoming as the children spread around it in groups of four or five, looking at fish, tins, vegetables. Dale was worried though: 'They're not drawing quickly enough, they're too tight, we must speed them up, move the groups more quickly.'

One five-year-old complained of another, 'He's scribbled over our picture'. Dale said 'You're not scribbling, you're making it better, aren't you?' 'I can't help it,' said the second child. 'I get excited and then I just scribble.' Later, Dale was more relaxed − and impressed. 'Look at them, look at what we're asking them to do. I couldn't do this, sit in a big store with everyone looking at what I'm drawing. I couldn't cope with it.'

He enjoyed the youngest children ('They're great − they'll draw anything'), because their enthusiasm and lack of inhibition is what he wants. Their drawings are snapshots, done directly, recording the basic information required: pure clean shapes without clutter. One nervous four-year-old, Louise, who had just started school, found she lost her worries as she lost herself in the drawing, moving from wide-eyed and disoriented to confident and smiling during an hour's work. We overheard a conversation: 'I was born out of God's hand.' 'I was born out of the ground like a mushroom.' 'Dale was born out of a painting.' Duncan said 'We'll have to go in a few minutes' and was told by a parent 'We've just got to do Wines and Spirits.'

The next day was the first day at school, and like a student on first teaching practice, Dale was under the weather with a cold that would later become worse as he got more and more tired. Here there is a feeling that he is as much a learner as the children are. He is learning, first, about the stress of teaching; how there is a huge gap between the words you say as *you* interpret them, and how *they* interpret them – and that neither interpretation is objectively correct. Speaker and listener collude in meanings, compromise in them, much as writer and reader collude (and compromise). If 'reading is complicity in the creative process' so is viewing and listening. Meanings are not delivered: not by teachers and not by writers, and not by artists. They are negotiated.

He is also learning about the strain on emotional and physical resources that teaching brings about; and his comment about Raphael and Picasso shows that he is learning from the children about his own subject. The children confirm what the masters had said.

'Have you got any emulsion? I think we'll splash some of that about. Really loosen them up. Big brushes.' Everything Dale says is about loosening children, about speed, about dumping inhibitions. He thinks fast himself: at coffee time on the first day in school, he has started to accept the teachers' doubts about the practicality of the children sharing their work to the extent of working from each other's drawings. The teachers don't believe the juniors will want to work with the infants' drawings.

The teachers have constant practical problems that Dale can mostly ignore: there's emulsion on the carpet, and Martyn has fallen in the paint – could they bring in old clothes for the rest of the fortnight? On the day of the Tesco visit, one parent helper dropped out, and they had to press Dale's car into service. Most of the practical matters have been arranged by Anne, a classroom ancillary, who works tirelessly and allows Dale room to explore.

By the end of the second day some large card has been used to make relief models of supermarket produce. The models stand out, casting shadows from the light of an overhead projector, and making silhouettes. Dale learns fast: about organising groups, about the precious nature of a child's work to herself, about children's perceptions of their own ability. And that is a central point: the residency is not just about the children learning by taking on a delivered curriculum. Learning is complicity in curriculum design, and delivery is therefore an inappropriate metaphor. The staff and the artist are learning, too – about pressures and practicalities, about an artistic way of thinking mixing with an institutional one.

Learning is what Dale paints for, much as Auden *wrote* to learn: 'How can I tell what I think till I see what I say?' Henry Moore made this point explicitly about drawing (quoted in the Mary Newland and Maurice Rubens pamphlet *Some Functions of Art in the Primary School* 1983): 'Drawing is a means of finding your way about things, and a way of experiencing more quickly certain tryouts and attempts.'

Dale challenges our fetish of mounts and displays, quoting Paul Klee to the effect that finished products are like the flowers on a tree: it is within the bark, the sap, and the roots that the real strength lies. 'Tell that to the NCC' one of us says. 'They'd see each flower as an attainment target, and never think about the bark or the sap.'

But for Dale things are never finished. When one of his large canvases, just unrolled from the back of the car, seems not to be going quite right, he says to the headteacher, Duncan, 'I think I might let the kids loose on that.' That's all very well, thinks the head, but the governors, the parents, even the TES photographer, all expect something finished, mounted, framed, on the walls. Even Dale falls into the trap at one point, saying a child has spoiled a piece of work. But he claims only to be interested in neatly rounding things off because otherwise he wouldn't sell his work: 'Framing and all that pays for my food ... it's nothing to do with the art but it helps you to see it properly, it stops the eye wandering elsewhere.'

The school accepts this point, but the gap between expecting some kind of finish, and the artist's extreme trust in the process, was the first misgiving on the part of the school. We wonder if Dale is enjoying it as much as he was: he relishes living on the line between order and chaos. But as someone has said, there are two great entities threatening the world: one is order, the other is chaos – and here the threat is from the chaos. And then, as if to keep him on his toes, a four-year-old takes Dale's breath away. Looking up suddenly from the bench where they've been working side by side, the boy asks: 'How big is your willy?'

But despite the slight shuddering in the week's foundations, in the school house one wall is covered by emulsioned paper which is in turn being covered by a pattern of abstract shapes, as small pieces of work are joined together, and to several independent observers this work is beautiful. These are panels, each 12×9 inches containing fish, crabs, fruit, vegetables. Some other shapes have been gained by drawing round images previously drawn on an OHP and now projected onto the wall.

In the next room, children are sawing a large piece of hardboard into small squares. They are reluctant to stop even when there's enough squares: again there's the pleasure in the process. Several visitors to the school during this period came away muttering 'We must do this at our school ... it's wonderful ... we must have an artist in residence.'

But all was not well. Duncan writes in notes only shown to the author months afterwards:

To us in the school the end of the first week came as a shock. Anne was away after working four solid working days with Dale. I stepped in to take her place and was immediately aware of how she had been holding things together. She had been the one dealing with the practical management; keeping tabs on four or five different group in various parts of the school house; providing more paint; tying aprons, cleaning hands, motivating and providing new ideas. She had been keeping the balance on the knife edge on which Dale loved to work.

But now the balance was upset, perhaps by my presence, true enough. But working among the children, I felt that the activities were deteriorating into worthlessness. The bright, clean ideas of the previous week seemed to be disappearing, overtaken by new ideas, without being completed. The new ideas were literally destroying the old. Pieces were being cut up, painted over, re-used. To say they were destroying the little heritage, the history of the week, sounds pretentious, but that's how it felt. If one of our aims was for the children to find out more about themselves and their surroundings then we were beginning to fail. There wasn't a commitment from the children, and for Dale and myself, all we could do was keep the lid on.

From Dale there were the first signs of irritation. A group of GCSE students had come to work with him. 'It's a waste of time. They're conditioned. I can't do anything with them, not in such a short time, they'd need a different scheme to address different strengths and weaknesses.'

We were all happy to see the end of the day. I went home very worried. We had learnt so much. Simply having someone so creative on the premises, someone not in the teaching profession, was invigorating. Dale challenged many of our thoughts about learning. His way of learning was by playing with ideas and materials. Cutting card. Painting on it. Turning it round. Taking the waste piece and using the negative shape. Scratching into the paint.

But as the Gulbenkian Report says 'Creative Work is not merely a question of playing with things, of randomness and chance. It has much to do with serious and sustained effort.' Dale's playfulness seemed infinitely creative to us and, as he says, 'How long does it take to produce art, fifty seconds, fifty years? How long does this serious and sustained effort have to last?' But, perhaps because of our institution, we needed some endings. Products.

On the subject of endings, Dale commented much later:

> Children have to learn when something is finished, but this is still *the* most difficult decision for *me* to make. Maybe they have to go over the top, almost destroy things, to know where their limits are. It's better to have problems about where to stop than about where to start! ... If I were to have stayed there at Tattingstone for six months, we would have had gains and losses all the time. Surely that's simply how life is. It's false, I feel, to cash your chips in when you're winning, take the work off them when *we* think it looks good (even though I did that in the supermarket).

'Anyway. I have to say' (Dale continued in notes given to me later) 'I didn't see a crisis at the end of the first week. If anything what I was attempting was over-ambitious for two weeks − given six months we could have made a giant, single artwork completely over all the school ... But if I didn't feel the crisis the school obviously did.'

And the school certainly did. It was so worried about it that it didn't even expose these worries till long after an initial article on the subject was written for the *Times Educational Supplement*. The school's feelings might have been put like this:

Dale's way was how pictures were made, yes, but also how pictures were never finished. Yet he did frame the pictures and exhibit them ('for his food'), and obviously felt great satisfaction about them. The children, on the other hand, didn't seem to be finishing anything. Each piece was being taken and used by the next group. And the children were questioning the point of doing anything. Certainly they were learning as they worked, but they weren't gaining the satisfaction of a finished piece of work in which they could re-live their experiences. They'd made a statement, and wanted to keep it.

FS commented later: Perhaps this is the crux of the process/product debate, in art, in writing, in dance, in drama, in music: the process is what is essential for the learning but the artist needs a product to reflect on. To be a base for the next attempt at learning, the next creative moment. He or she needs that rest to reflect, when there must be no more movement, while we *think*, both about what we've done and about what we might do next. Dale is worried that 'product ' is too much a word from marketing; art he says is a 'spiritual' activity. But there are objects, whether we like it or not.

Duncan continues: I spent the Friday evening talking things over with Jenny (his wife). I felt sure I had to change the whole mood of the residency, but how would Dale take it? And how was it best done? By the end of the evening we'd decided to go in on the Saturday to clear things up, mount some work and set up a print shop for the following week. Dale worked a lot with lino cuts and I wanted the children to use their Tesco drawings in this way. We decided that Dale would concentrate his work into one room with one group of children while Anne would work with the rest. This way Dale and Anne would be able to focus their one activity in one place. The children would see a slowly growing set of prints, and while they would be able to build on their ideas by changing and merging colours, or by cutting away at the block itself, they would still keep their images of their earlier work.

I felt much better now that there was more order about the building. The decision was right for the school. (Dale says this sentence is 'very dodgy'.) If the parents were to support our art work, we must have something to show at the end. ('So,' asks Dale rhetorically, 'we let the children play football at lunchtime because we're expecting to produce professional footballers, rather than because it's a means of exercise?')

What we'd done over the weekend had to over-ride the possibility of Dale not accepting the decision. I hadn't spoken to him about it. This may have been cowardice on my part but I had the feeling that when he saw everything prepared for the following week he would see my reasoning. This was of course a *fait accompli*, and he had little choice. Despite his way of working, continually cutting, changing, he did work in a clean and tidy environment. A printer has to, and I knew he'd found the end of the first week difficult, and was tired and over-stretched.

Monday morning. Anne had been worrying all weekend too and was grateful for the new plans. Dale arrived, and he too seemed quite happy with things, although I think I caught him smiling at an unfinished painting I had strip-mounted with black paper in my efforts on Saturday to restore order. As the second week progressed, beautiful prints started to emerge. Some were figurative: speckled cakes and strangely distorted bottles; others purely abstract, with shapes floating in space. Dale says: 'I know why beautiful prints emerged. It is all to do with the different relationship the viewers have with paintings and prints – prints are a quicker experience, they have flat, pure colour vignetted by white paper, they don't threaten the space of the viewer, they are more acceptable to the eye.'

We spent the last afternoon all together, exchanging presents and saying goodbye. We had begun the residency hoping the children would be able to share their work without being possessive or protective. In many ways this hadn't worked (concludes Duncan Allan), but on that last afternoon there was a great satisfaction in what we had all achieved.

The residency was financed by Eastern Arts, and cost £80 per day plus expenses: fee, materials, travel etc. And the reason we under-value the arts is because they show up our normal day-to-day practice in schools for the time-wasting, stalling nonsense it often is: 'I've finished.' 'Well, colour it in ... write a poem about it ... Copy it out ... Measure it.'

The head felt unsettled by what he'd learnt. What now? Back to boring stuff out of a book? He had begun to question everything he did in school. 'People come to make sure children are "on task", are they doing their sums, are we checking our lists right – and that's all shown up for what it is by an experience like this. Dale said, "What do you do with these young ones all day? You give them something and it's finished in five seconds and you can't fault it?" Some of the answers to that question were shaming.'

Was it worth it? Certainly for Louise, learning confidence by the minute, and James, boldly drawing bananas and oranges on the floor of Tesco, it was. And for Matthew, who cried as Dale drove off for the last time.

And to the parents, Dale brought an opening of windows, a snatched look at a new country. He gained a glimpse of what education is like in a system, as opposed to the gloriously luxurious moment on your own in a studio.

It was also worth it for a visiting head, who murmured, almost to himself, 'Will this sort of glory carry on when the National Curriculum's fully in place?' And for the head of Tattingstone, shaken up, and put down with his mind and heart changed, it'll turn out to have effects that he hasn't dreamed of yet.

Though this wasn't quite what the schools minister meant, it was great to see the arts in the market place: pictures off walls, and growing, rapidly, on floors and tables, as teachers, children, parents and artist came to understand one another and their shared medium. And much of the learning, of course, was in getting through the crisis of the end of the first week, when there was a temporary resolution of the product/process debate; when someone at least needed something finished, in a kind of order, so he could see where they all might go next.

CHAPTER 5

And I Celebrate All Rhythms

with Brigida Martino

Dance should come first. It stands alongside music as the primal
form of expression and, still today, as the form of expression that
most humans can use. As Mr D'Arcy sneered, 'Every savage can
dance.'

I move across the floor, slowly, suddenly turning, spiky and ridged. I walk
towards the wall. The music stops. I freeze. I punch, kick, turn and stretch
in silence.

(*Girl, 9*)

When I dance, I can be me. I know that sounds pretentious. But I can
be who I think I am. (Yes, I know that's not necessarily me!) I can even
be the sexual person I am, without frightening the horses, which I can't
normally, except in private. I can be aggressive, I can be cajoling, I can
laugh, I can sing, I can be me.

(*Adult, age not disclosed*)

My dance and how I relate it with the children and teach has enhanced my
perception and understanding of many, many things in life.

(*Another adult*)

James Berry, in the title poem of his collection *When I Dance*
writes:

> ...when I dance
> O music expands my hearing
> And it wants no mathematics,
> It wants no thinking, no speaking,
> It only wants all my feeling
> In with animation of face ...

79

The poem ends 'And I celebrate all rhythms'.

From these examples, we might judge that dancing is an expressive mode, an art, in which all of us feel our nature is expressed. In 1969, I was a probationary teacher on an inservice dance course in Stevenage, and I thought then that my fear, my reluctance to take a prominent part in the course was due to physical clumsiness: I have never been adept at games or anything requiring motor skill, whether large or small. I was certainly anxious about my leotarded colleagues being flames or aspiration and roses all around the school hall. I spent much of the time half hiding with a Park Drive staining the palms of my hands, and thinking of the next pint.

At the beginning of the last morning, the tutor, a powerful person from Balls Park College (now part of the University of Hertfordshire) told us that by the end of that day we were to make 'a statement about our feelings about this course in dance'. I decided to go for the (to me, then) rare sincerity option. After some thought, I crouched down, making myself as small as possible, 'like' as we say to children 'a hedgehog'. I rocked from side to side; then, very slowly, I raised my eyes and looked all around the room: at everything: the tutor, the flames, the crocuses, the aspiration. I caught sight of the fields outside the school hall, and the freedom they poignantly represented, and brushed them conscientiously from my mind.

I spent some moments rocking and looking, my eyes (I assumed at the time) wide with apprehension, even fear. That was, after all, how I felt. Then I went sadly back to my rocking position, a beaten man who had looked and found himself wanting in the face of such ambitious company.

The tutor came by and kicked me gently on the bottom. She said 'You're not putting much effort into this.'

One point of this story is to show that even I could conceive of dance – well, movement anyway – as a vehicle for my feelings. But also the reason for my failure (as perceived by all the participants) wasn't only my clumsiness but also my unwillingness to show my feelings. And yet *my unwillingness to show my feelings was the important part of my feelings at the time*. I was showing my feelings, all too clearly. Thus the incident made me wary of sixties liberals who asked us to express ourselves – and then told us off when we did and our feelings didn't match up to what they thought they should be.

Another, more important, lesson the incident taught me was that in all art there is tension between technique and feeling. Pure sincerity is not nearly enough. Michael Baldwin goes so far as to say that 'technique ... is half of any poet's religion', and no doubt this follows for the other arts. Seurat said somewhere – I read it in a gallery brochure – 'they see poetry in what I have done. No, I apply my method, and that is all there is to it'.

Of course, this is an extreme view. Maybe Seamus Heaney comes close to the truth when he says that 'craft is what you can learn from other verse' (read paintings, music, drama, dance); 'technique ... involves ... a definition of a stance towards life'. Technique, then, is a powerful mix of method and feeling. The paradox is that working on technique releases, or educates us about, the feeling. That is the value of obscurity in art: the intellectual effort required allows the work to have its emotional effect on us. Working towards the solution of a technical problem helps us to shape, to make public, the work's emotion. Without the technical problem and the effort required, the result would be shapeless and would have a sentimental effect. This is why tyro art strikes us as weak: the feeling is there, but the technical structure is unformed.

To look through manifestations of a cultural view of what art is: entries for a national poetry competition, paintings done for local art exhibitions, amateur dramatics, is to be aware that for most people sincerity is all, and technique doesn't come into the reckoning. My technique-less sincerity struck the teacher as lack of effort. But there had been no emphasis on technique in the course, only on self-expression. And I was certainly expressing myself.

The massive claims made by Berry, the anonymous adults and the child quoted above don't go for all dance, of course. Here is an account of a presentation by a secondary school:

> All the girls (and they are all girls) are wearing identical uniforms, blue and yellow tops and skirts. To loud rock (pop really) music, they move identically: to some extent, the success to which they move identically is the measure of their success. For example, they throw their heads and shoulders back, and swoop their hair forward. Perfect: they all arrive at the head down position simultaneously. Or they swing their arms in front of their legs, meanwhile somehow, moving to one side: clever as hell, and identical ... This is an extremely polished performance, and I am reminded of countless Top of the Pops programmes.

Children, my friend Brigida says later, are naturally expressive, but we demand in situations like this what she calls 'a straight line approach ... conformity'. She also comments quietly on the inappropriately sexual nature of the performance.

And I remember country dancing at primary school: thousands of children well-practised in Brighton Camp or whatever, all met together on a sports field.

Although dance is as old as humankind, it has a very recent history as a part of the curriculum in primary schools. This is partly because it is a joy one has to kiss as it flies. It can't be triple-mounted and pinned on the wall, it can't even be written down, despite Laban's efforts, as music can. Dance is resistant to being pinned. It won't wriggle on the page. Its dynamics are time and the fleeting moment. This may be a weakness educationally, but it is also a strength because, in its process-emphasis, it concentrates the mind on the moment and helps us escape, however briefly, from the tyranny of the target.

Although recently there has been a new emphasis on production and performance, at least in part because of the National Curriculum's emphasis on measurable outcomes, it is in its ability to help individuals of very various levels of ability to understand themselves and their relationship to the space around them and other individuals that dance has its educational and expressive power. This is the view of this chapter.

Dance was late on the scene as a curricular art. In schools it had been an inheritor, till the 1960s, of the PE tradition: drill, physical training/education, gymnastics, movement. Dance was taught, if it was taught at all, by the PE teachers, not those concerned with aesthetics. Depressingly, in Tickle's 1987 book with the inviting title *The Arts in Education – Some Research Studies* there are only three index entries for dance, and none of them yields anything of substance. There are excellent chapters on Art, Drama, Poetry and Music, as well as provocative theoretical essays (especially by Clem Adelman) – but nothing on Dance at all. And this is in a book that stands up at several points for a radical view of teaching.

Anna Haynes, in her essay 'Changing Perspectives in Dance Education' in Peter Abbs' 1987 book *Living Powers*, has provided a clear and very useful history of dance education in the twentieth century. She points out the dilemma that affects all the arts and how 'in dance, the split between the two [views] was unnecessarily sharp'.

> There was a major contention over 'product' versus 'process' ... those committed to establishing a formal aesthetic stressed technique, expertise, performance ... those committed to the individual development of their pupils placed emphasis on process and feeling, on exploratory work, with the notion of performance in the background ...

While I am saddened by the polarisation of views here, since I assume that formalists and expressionists have much to teach each other, I also note that those of us concerned with schools can't but be concerned with 'the individual development of their pupils' – above all else, and especially above the performance of the best of those pupils while the rest watch.

This chapter is concerned with adult education – in the shape of INSET for teachers – as well as the education of children, and as such is unique in this book. But all the arts teach adults as well as children. And a model for schooling that insists on delivery, which implicitly assumes that teachers have had education and that children need it, falsifies the nature of human reality as we know it. If children have a right to learn, so do teachers; and if teachers stop learning, so will the children. Or, more exactly, they will continue to learn, but not what the teachers try to teach them.

In contrast to both the country dancing and the girls' robotic pop in the secondary school, Brigida Martino is teaching a class of mixed top juniors (Y5 and 6) in a dance lesson watched by a group of twenty teachers on a course. Brigida is an experienced teacher with an initial qualification (Cert Ed) in secondary science. She has spent the last ten years at this school in Ipswich (Downing CP) but with a break to teach in Canada. She has also taught in Pakistan.

The teachers are sitting round the edge of the hall on small blue plastic chairs, holding mugs of tea and instant coffee. It is late October, and Brigida has known these children for about six weeks. This is their first intensive experience of dance. She has known some of the teachers well for a long time, others she has just met. It is 4.30 when she says to the children: 'You are going to get up slowly into a stretch ... where are you looking Ben? ... slowly, slowly ... Don't forget your point of focus ...

Now, stretch together, curve together, but don't touch.'

After a minute, Brigida gets two of the children to demonstrate. Two others grin satirically at each other. Their teacher is holding a cymbal, which she uses to stop or start something. But then all the children, including the two boys who look as if they don't want to be involved, present curved shapes that are fuller, stronger than their first attempts. The work develops for some ten minutes. One child, annoyed with herself, starts again. Another practises his shape. You'd think he was unaware of the adults around the walls of his school hall.

Then the children listen to some slow, curvy music. In fact, later investigation shows it's the slow movement of the Aaron Copland clarinet concerto. 'Start comfortable,' says Brigida, 'like cats are by the fire ... when you get to your stretch place, just stop ...' Three children demonstrate their work so far. Three more teachers arrive, apologising. But why should they? Teachers are expected to improve their work, to get better, at the end of an exhausting day. They pour tea, looking over their shoulders into the hall, anxious about what they might have missed. They sit down with little spiral notebooks on their knees and start scribbling immediately. Whether the arts are about form or expression, technique or emotion, product or process, teachers are expected to learn about them in little grabbed moments after school, that are euphemistically called twilight sessions.

The children do their curvy catlike movements again. Ella is praised for her different (hunched) start. She is distinguishable from her friends in other ways: she clearly doesn't want to show off her work in front of everyone: she is genuinely interested in the process, the learning, the experience, in the physical sensations the work produces. She is getting on with things. Her eyes lock out the occasional misbehaviour, the odd sarcastic glance.

Three more teachers arrive. One carries a pile of maths exercise books – surely she is not going to do her marking now? – and another a copy of a DES report she is, it turns out, half way through. Another is to show me later some writing her children have done.

Who else covers as much human learning experience in a single day as a primary school teacher? The technology of bridge building. A story about a Viking child. A hymn affirming the Christian faith ('Firmly I believe and truly') and music and drama affirming other faiths. A game of football, a game of netball. Some measurement. And none of this mentions the psychology, the sociology, the history, the research methods, the management they need. And now some dance.

Two boys – not the satirists – are more clumsy, less flowing than everyone else. They are put off by the new entries. Ella is hunched up, and her curves use space all around her, not just in front and at the side. She always starts differently, as though she knows what Ezra Pound knew – that the only way of making art is to make it new, even when (as we must) we use the accumulated forms and understanding of the past. She is a quiet, unobtrusive girl. Maybe she enjoys learning, maybe she merely plays the school game.

Brigida then goes around, picking out good work and praising it. 'Much more interesting' is a phrase she uses to avoid 'good' or 'better' or 'best'. But the children know. I looked at Brigida's lesson notes. They are divided into seven sections: Idea, Since last time, Aim, Accompaniment, Warm-Up, Main Emphasis and Conclusion. Under Idea she has written 'Stretch and Curl'; Since last time, 'The children will have spent some time observing kittens/cats and their movements, preparation for this lesson will have been through all the areas of the curriculum'; her Aim was 'contrast'; the Accompaniment the Copland Concerto. Under Main Emphasis, Brigida has written:

Levels → rise/fall/sink: reacting towards a point
Shape → tensions → relaxed, comfortable, secure or strange, like elastic. How does your body feel?
Conclusion: Children to work in groups for (a) stretch and curl together and (b) stretch and curl opposite.

What emerges from this is how even an experienced and, it must be said, expert teacher like Brigida still makes detailed preparatory notes for her teaching. There is no hint of letting the ideas arise when you get to the hall: she has clear aims in her mind.

The Tube of Smarties is an exercise that Brigida uses to get the children out of the hall. It is a piece of skippy, jaunty music that provides a relaxation after the intense work that constitutes the main part of the lesson. The children skip away to the library up the stairs, where they have left their outer clothes, and where their parents are now congregating, and she is left with the teachers. This, she says, is the most difficult moment. She approaches them now with an artificial confidence. The temperature has dropped in two minutes. We need the children, it seems, and in-service sessions that include them have a warmth and a strength that normal INSET doesn't have. They also have a practicality – we can see the INSET provider coping with the problems we cope with day by day – that flipcharts and fat felt tip pens don't have.

The teachers look back warily, already expressing themselves in movement and expression, without thinking about it: defensiveness, anxiety. Brigida is going to ask the teachers to try the different activities.

There is a short discussion in the corner of the hall, which I don't hear. They take off shoes and socks and cardigans and jumpers. They loosen up. They giggle. They wiggle their toes, roll. 'What I do for this bloody profession!' 'And after a day like today!' 'If my class could see me now!' Brigida smiles, controls it all with her drum. Bang! Clumsily quarter-undressed they wait, frozen, for her next command.

Then in small groups they explore different percussion movements. A clout on the drum: some fall, and lie still, others snap round, fix an aggressive glare on someone. A brushed noise, and they mimic it with a gentle waving movement. A series of beats, and they move jerkily at different levels round the hall, like jumping jack crackers. It is impressive how unselfconscious they suddenly are. Maybe the tensest people can use dance to relax. Anyway, Brigida supplies a good atmosphere for fun, for laughter, and a task: she gave them percussion instruments. 'They had to work with that instrument,' she said later.

A group with a maracas improvised on the theme of a rattlesnake. Another group, using drums, homed in on gunshot. The castanets led to a follow-my-leader game.

'Any group want to share?' she says later, using that progressive's euphemism for 'display', or even 'show off', when the teachers have been asked to put their work into groups. I think that maybe if I'd known Brigida twenty-two years ago, instead of the fierce woman from Balls Park, I'd be a different person now: more relaxed with my body, less puritanical perhaps. It is also impressive how a group of individuals occupied all day with thirty human beings largely dependent on them can work like this at 4.30pm.

The rattlesnake group is willing to share. They move, bend, in swirling columns, and look each other in the eye, dismissively. They threaten, rise, subside, arms copying the movements of their bodies and somehow, it seems, the movement of the whole column. The ratchety noise goes on behind. This is much more socially demanding than courses on writing, say, where you can not only avoid each other but the task – by pretending to write, or by making notes of ideas for writing, instead of writing yourself.

Here the teachers have to move, and this is very exposing of perceived physical and imaginative deficiencies. Also, in looking in a stranger's eyes you have to take a risk. They let the rattling noise of the wooden instrument lead them in a sinuous, threatening, snaky motion. Another group is dancing a fight. 'Go on, get 'em on the floor! That's it, Mrs Rainbow!' shouts Brigida. Behaviour that is illegitimate on the playground, in the hall, in the classroom, at the tea table is all kosher here. They crowd round a victim who is slowly crushed in a stylised street fight. Those of us watching admiringly observe placid Mrs Rainbow beat a stranger to death on the hall floor.

Later in the course this violence becomes even more prominent as the children mime anger in front of twenty-odd teachers and a few parents. Fists jerk upwards in parodies of fascist rallies or the lowest extremes of football fan behaviour. When Brigida introduces some clipped, sharp brutal music, the children express violence in a more controlled way: they keep their focus, for example; one group makes an angry sculpture, and it has a frightening totalitarian feel to it, like something in Orwell's *1984*, like Hitler and Stalin's approved art, like, again, football violence.

I am reminded of a letter a publisher sent me. I had produced an anthology of poems for children (*This Way That Way*). A headteacher wrote that unless the publishers sent her a prepaid label she would burn the books because they encouraged violence. The reasons were four poems: two playground rhymes about smacking children, this one that children everywhere in the English-speaking world have versions of:

I'm telling Miss on you
You dirty kangaroo
I'll kick you up the chimney pot
And make you black and blue.

and this poem of mine, 'The Fight':

There's a fight on the playground today –
Two big boys from Mr Magee's
Are knocking the daylights out of each other
Under the trees.

The girls are silent and staring
And Clare whispers 'Stop it Paul'
As the fighting gets wilder, and feet jab out
And fingers maul.

I watch, and I'm glad it's not Joe
And me in that horrible space –
Not my stomach winded, not my nose bleeding,
Not my burning face.

The sky is bright. Two planes fly
Out from the base, while one
Boy holds the other down with his knee
And breathes 'You done?'

There's a fight on the playground today –
Paul Topple from Mr Magee's
Is crushing the daylights out of John Randall
Under the trees.

I sometimes ask children to write about violence and hatred, and teachers object. That isn't very nice. I'm not sure you should do that. Aren't you encouraging violence?

What are we protecting here? We are aware of the potential violence in us, the spurts of hatred, when perhaps we are carved up on a roundabout or a boss makes a sarcastic remark about us. Dance allows us – as poetry does, and all the arts – to respond with that sincere anger, but without hurting anyone. It allows us access to even more serious hatreds: the times in relationships when we suffer the long dark night that might, for all we know, go on forever. If we cannot deal with these feelings in our artistic experiences, where can we deal with them?

In the street, or the pub, probably, or the home. Art can rehearse the worst of our feelings in a shaped way – and those who would relegate art below technology, science, business studies and industrial awareness bear a responsibility for how our streets, homes and pubs will be in the next century.

Brigida says that there 'is less control of the risk in dance than there is in other arts ... It is not only the shape, but the movement into the shape that offers glimpses into the person'. (Glimpses into the person! Is that why I was shy? Poems offers glimpses, of course – but not in my presence. I don't like people reading my poems while I'm there.)

It's all a risk for another reason; all the tools, pens, pencils, paper, brushes, word processors, tape recorders, dictaphones, musical instruments have been taken away. All that is there is a body and a space. Perhaps that is partly why I don't get up despite Brigida's requests. I raise my private notebook as if to plead an excuse. Admittedly, when we sing, we are only using our bodies. But there is usually the support of a piano or a guitar. There is a particular sort of vulnerability when we dance.

These children have written notes for poems. They are on the tables at the side of the hall, and I glance at them as the teachers' fight comes to an end:

An angry instrument

a quick snap of your eyes
collapse like dominoes
stamp your feet hard
go out of control
be mean and sly
quick and scramble
freeze

A loving instrument

slide gently across the smooth brown floor
slow like a snail
flow like a bubble
swift like a leaf
twist like a spinning top
tiptoe to the left
creep behind another person

When I am angry I feel like a whirlpool

damaging everything in my path.
I feel like a falcon trying to kill its prey.

Brigida comments that dance emphasises the differences in our personalities: 'I see things this way, you that ... The children move towards each other, there's an interaction, then they separate ... Life can be like that.'

From Brigida's lesson notes, I learn that the 'tight, angular, sharp angry movements' were accompanied by 'White Snake'; and that the gentler movements by the second movement of the Beethoven Fifth Piano Concerto (which enabled Seamus Heaney's pupils to 'trip/To fall into themselves unknowingly' in his poem 'The Play Way', from his first collection, *Death of a Naturalist* 1966)

The session closes with Brigida suggesting that the teachers take one of the activities and try it with their own classes. 'The problem,' she says to me afterwards, 'is not to make the demo lesson so slick, so impressive that the teachers shy away. The idea is "You can do this and you owe it to the children you teach."'

This work is teaching things that are often neglected in our schools. For example, it is making demands on non-verbal expressive skills. It is a listening and a telling with the whole body.

The following week it emerges that a teacher called Richard from another school has tried the anger motif. 'I have a background in country dancing,' he says. 'Very structured ... the kids were embarrassed at first ... I heard one of them say "This is going to be embarrassing!"' But he was 'amazed and delighted' by the children's reaction; they were at ease and working within minutes.

At the beginning of the third session, the children come in with proud faces and walks. They love demonstrating their work. The authority's adviser is here, and they know how good their teacher is, and why they're here. The boys who sneered at the beginning of the first session are now completely involved. Ella anticipates the lesson with her usual unaffected commitment. Her mother, still dressed for the shop where she works, and her little brother from the nursery have arrived. Outside the dark is clean; across the courtyard cleaners are framed in bright classrooms; no fog today. Brigida asks them to think about the writing they did this morning. 'We're going to play the music we played when you were writing.'

Every teacher concentrates. The music is clear in the cold snowy November air. Some might say that the music – Pictures at an Exhibition – is being devalued used in this way. But it isn't a holy thing, a Grecian Urn, to be gazed at and worshipped. It is part of life, to be used, like a box or a meal or a glass of wine.

Lee gazes at Paul as he moves around, Paul's eyes fixed ahead. Brigida says: 'I want you to hide (cymbal) in another way (cymbal), and another (cymbal), and another (cymbal).' This shows (she says to me later) that there are many right ways; you aren't looking for a single correct way in dance, or in any of the arts. That is why the notion of training is inappropriate for this kind of work. It says there is a right way, the teacher knows it, so listen. Watch. Do what I say.

Someone has written during the day

Hiding in a brown bin from footsteps coming towards me in the dark.
Hiding from fireworks in the darkness.
Hiding from footsteps of man in the deep yellow blazing sunlight.

Gemma moves towards the evading Linda. They are cats and prey: not on all fours, but twisting and turning at all levels, tip-toe, moving upwards, downwards, forwards and backwards. Nicola's left leg is bent, her arms expressive and her arms flowing. Matthew (a very disturbed boy, distracted suddenly by his father's sudden desertion of his mother, and further by his mother's equally sudden new liaison) is moving forward expressively. 'That's gorgeous!' says the adviser. Matthew manages not to smile up at her, to keep his work going. Marie is relishing the setting. She finishes with her left arm spread out.

Only Daniel is caught in the four-legged cat thing, and as a result, he looks more like Tom from Tom and Jerry than he does like a cat: though, paradoxically, Tom never walks on all fours! What I mean is that Daniel is like a hand-me-down cliché of a cat, obsessed with shape, photographic exactness, rather than feeling and expression. The others are freer, getting the impressions of a cat, the feelings, the sense of cattiness through the sweeps of their arms and legs, the curve of their bodies.

At the fourth session, which got off to a late start, the children came in wearing untemplated cat and mouse masks. These have been made in art sessions when cat poems have been read: 'Milk for the Cat' by Harold Munro, for example; and 'Fourteen Ways of Touching the Peter' by George Macbeth.

A girl has written a haiku:

Cat with angry look
with back arching like a
rainbow without colours.

and another child has a scribbled note:

It moves slowly and softly, a little bit at a time . . .

'Hide,' said Brigida to the mouse group. 'Don't let your partner hear you.' They seemed less awed than usual, and there is less tension in the atmosphere. This is, of course, great if it means that the children are more relaxed, but bad if they care less. Does art always require some tension? The more relaxed atmosphere may have something to do with the masks. If we are hiding, we can more securely be ourselves. A sudden technical hitch with the music dissipates more tension.

'Go strong again.' The children use their own ideas as starting points, and these ideas are often clichés: hands and arms over faces, crouched positions. It is then the teacher's task to give options without curtailing the children's autonomy. This is a common problem in teaching the arts: the charismatic teacher will all too often teach children by getting them to produce objects, whether poems, pictures, music or movement all too like her own.

Brigida gave me notes from her plans for other lessons on this theme:

I often get them to use an object: a chair, a piece of newspaper, or cloth, a stage block. These objects then become part of the dance, once the children come out of hiding, so they represent the other. For example, the newspaper can become the focus for anger so that it is tossed, ripped, destroyed; and it can be gently brought together again in the form the child wants. This can reflect the child's experience of being bullied or of being a bully; or of some fear that they want to destroy. Building it up again is determined by the child, and gives power, autonomy. I have tried this in classes and been amazed at the children's response. I recall one child who ripped the newspaper into bits, threw them in the air and stood with her arms folded. This was about bullying and it was happening to her! I have linked this lesson with RE. When doing the Good Samaritan, children have chosen cloth to be the rock the robbers hide behind. It then became the wounded man. I was moved by the tenderness of those two children, two boys.

Using the other persons: we often hide behind others and emerge when we judge it is safe to do so. I think of Adam hiding behind Eve, the child saying 'He told me to ... ' This can be used in this lesson.

The whole theme of hiding can be developed. Children can be shown that they do hide, and helped to identify what they are hiding from. Dance can give them an opportunity to emerge. Step out. We can spend our lives as adults in hiding behind our social upbringing, education, etc. By hiding we fail to grow, to step out.

Despite the worries about copying Miss's ideas, the children have significant autonomy, and Brigida tells them not to look at her. 'I feel this seeks teacher approval.' This lessens autonomy, because it makes the teacher the sole audience, rather than the child's feelings and technique.

What is missing here, Brigida says to me later, is any evidence that I'm concerned with how the children perceive the dance lesson. I've not looked for their language about dance. Indeed, one way of increasing autonomy would be to interview a child about the experience.

In untemplated dance, the children learn about themselves. They 'fall into themselves/Unknowingly ...' But I take Brigida's point: how would they talk about it?

CHAPTER 6

Why Don't They Teach Us to Dance?

with Brigida Martino

Three years later Brigida was doing a part-time MA at the University of East Anglia and had decided to study dance in school for her dissertation. 'It's a shame' she said to me 'that the research is taking over my thesis ... I have to keep questioning my research methodology, and I haven't time or space to concentrate with what really obsesses me, teaching dance.' I had noted this effect before. Researching frequently causes research and its problems – such as access, objectivity, methodology, fairness, readability – to become the substantive issue instead of what started out as the main focus: poetry or the management of schools. Here it was happening to the dance. In an article I wrote in 1988 the title gave the game away: 'Talking about Teaching Poetry'. I wanted to write about poetry, but first the teaching, and then the talking – and then the writing! – all got in the way.

Brigida found the research got in the way of the teaching and the dance. 'But I had grown up a bit, I think. I knew now I wanted the children to look into their dance lesson, to have something to say about it, to evaluate themselves. I wanted them to respond, to use the language of dance, to talk about it. A lot of what was coming out of the National Curriculum was about children using the language of their arts, and I suddenly realised that I hadn't asked the children to talk about the dance at all.

'So Paul, one of the fathers, made videos of two lessons, so that the children could observe some of their work, and I could find out what they thought of what I was doing with them in dance. As one of the children, Robin, said, ''You can't see yourself if you don't have the film – you can see

94

your pictures, you can see your poems, but you can't see your dance."'

Robin is right: you can step out of time spent on a picture or a poem and reflect on it, evaluate it, enjoy it. Dance, though, which lives like music precariously in time, needs to be held up by film to be enjoyed by the dancers as art.

Brigida asked Suffolk's Advisor for the Performing Arts, Scilla Dyke, what a primary dance lesson should look like:

> There should be three sections within each session. You need to have a warm-up/choreographic composition type element so that they're getting their bodies ready to move properly, an evaluative, appreciation element and an element of performance. The performance, the sharing takes place both during the making, and after . . .

What follows comes from Brigida's notes, drafted while looking at the video and talking to Scilla Dyke. It was later part of an MA thesis.

'Ready and moving, really rapidly!' The warm up with its opening, commanding words jolts the children into obedience. They prepare bodies, getting them moving to the beat of the drum, the clash of the cymbal. I'm in control of it all, and there's the usual feeling of exhilaration as I begin a dance lesson – then I remember this is just a video. Later, the camera frames Christopher as he responds to the 'How are you falling' call accompanied by the cymbal. The slow button on the remote control is down, giving time for observation of the body in movement.

Christopher leads with his left hand, moving it towards the front of his body. He lifts it up to his tilting head. The fingers are open, their tips his focus. I note how conscientiously he holds this focus. Then, smoothly, he turns away from the camera moving to the floor, transferring his weight onto the left knee. His arm opens, dabs out and up as if to steady himself. As he falls his right arm supports his folding body. Opening out, he turns to face the camera, eyes looking towards the white ceiling. His fingers seem to brush briefly across his lips. He draws legs together, and with slow weaving movements, his fingers lead his body into a closed shape.

This is nine seconds transcribed during the warm up. Later he watches the video and I tell him 'Watch what you do' and we both look towards the screen. I say 'What do you think of that?'

'Exciting'

'What were you doing?'

I re-run this brief extract. The last digit on the counter turns seven times. He watches, chews on the white paper in his mouth. I glance at his blank, anxious eyes. What does Miss want of me?

We are in the TV room at the school, used for watching schools' programmes and by the peripatetic music teachers: brass, cello, violin, guitar. There's always been a lot of music here, because a previous music teacher was married to one of the advisors. They're both retired, but the effects of their generosity remain. Christopher has put an empty guitar case on the floor so he can sit down.

'What were you doing?'

'Dunno ... Dunno.'

At times like this, FS comments, I become a nihilist: perhaps there is nothing to be learnt from these moments, these scraps of data. 'Exciting' here is merely a teacher-oriented response, what Christopher thinks Brigida wants to hear. It means nothing except 'I want to please you but I don't know how, Miss', which is what children mean a good deal of the time in schools – as when the boy in Sandra's first drama lesson (Chapter 7) puts his hand up, though he has nothing to say.

I recall a book of poems I reviewed ten years ago where everything was reduced to nothing. Every image seemed to be round like a 0: apples, peas, moonheads, golfballs. Looking at videos of children, and listening to their comments on them, often seems like that, or like a scrap of dialogue from a sub-Beckett play. We can search and search, turn the dead stones over again and again and again, but there is nothing there.

I was recently involved with a book of case studies about education, and a reviewer commented that all the teaching described in the book seemed to go suspiciously well. He was hinting that some of the authors had made it up. In the case of Christopher's conversation, Brigida, it seems, was facing utter failure. It is authentic, as even that reviewer would have known: 'What did you say?' 'Nothing.' 'I thought you ...' 'No.' 'Don't you feel ...?' 'Not really ...'

Brigida continues: I push for a response. 'Can you describe

your movements?' I stop the video. His image becomes blurred. He is silent and continues to chew, looking towards the screen.

'How would you describe that?'

'I didn't make much noise when I fall down to the ground.'

'Can you remember what you were thinking about?'

On the screen he twists, turns, spins. He pauses briefly in the TV room.

'It's difficult to remember.'

'Yes, it is. So you can't remember what you were thinking about?'

'No.'

There is a moment of silence and I try again as images flick before us.

'How would you describe your movements?'

'Mostly close together. Some of the time big movements, but most of the time little movements.'

'Is there anything else you'd like to say about it?'

'No, not really.'

'Let me wind this back. How would you describe those movements to someone?'

'Making my body floppy, weak so I've got my body going down to the floor. When there is a big bang I just go down gently.'

'So what are you actually doing when you're moving here?'

I press the button for the last time. His captured movements are before us again. In the dark room he shrugs slightly. After five years of seeking teacher attention, he now has riches of it, intense and demanding, and it is too much for him.

'Gently, soft, weak . . .?' he asks.

FS comments: It is odd this, asking children what they think of our lessons. The aesthetic theorists never ask children what art's about. But neither do the rest of us: how did Brigida imagine Christopher would give her any data, when nobody in his school career had ever asked him about what he'd just been taught? What can Christopher imagine? No wonder he clams up. When he remarks 'When there is a big bang I just go down gently' he may well be interpreting this odd situation as Brigida's attempt to get him to see what was wrong with his performance: he thinks she's implying there's a 'wrong' gap between 'big bang' and 'gently', though she isn't implying this at all. She genuinely values what he says, but because of past experience, he can't grasp this. If a teacher questions him in anything like an intense way, he moves into 'being disciplined' mode: 'I'm being told off'.

Perhaps 'schools are places of mystery' as a government minister is fond of saying at the moment, and we are suffering from the gap between teachers and parents because of that gap, and our failure to bridge it. So said Brigida (or something like it) later. This is all a mystery to the child, certainly. So often we ask children to do something, but don't tell them why. And then, occasionally, the child perceives the world, to a greater or lesser degree, as insane.

> A boy in Preston twenty years ago comes to the teacher's desk with his writing finished. It seems to be all right, except that there is a comma after every word. 'Why have you done that, Richard?' asks the teacher. 'Sir, I breathed – '. (story from Geoff Southworth)

These are like children's famous misunderstandings of hymns and prayers ('My hope to follow Julie'; 'Our Father which art in Heaven, Harold be Thy name') only arguably of more educational significance. Christopher has never learned in five years at school that teachers want to know what he thinks about his work. Now one really does, for, it must be said, research purposes – and Christopher is baffled.

Brigida writes: The warm up on the video continues. The children jump, turn, tumble, warming up their bodies, warming up their minds to bring out movements that may be taken into the composition. The video light flashes on. I fast forward the tape to the composition element: the speed, skid, crash and stop part, which has its roots in the classroom theme of Road Safety and is the third of three lessons. The children on the screen gather round the teacher, me, by the stage.

My voice is saying: ' ... it's four beats on the counter. It's very, very short. It's the speed of the car, it's the skid and it's the crash, so you're going to work individually first and then you're going to work in groups. Okay, listen to it. Here we go.'

The speeding car cracks the silence of the hall. Sound roaring through a crescendo, horn full blast, brakes alert. 'That's the speed.' Wheels skidding, sliding. A car out of control. 'That's the skid.' An explosion, glass shatters, splinters and falls. 'The crash.

Okay, so you've got speed, skid, crash, skid, crash. That's the sequence.'

There had been some poems written the day before. It's odd how drama, dance, painting, drawing feel tarnished when touched by the wider curriculum, like road safety, while poetry mucks its hands with anything . . .

A muddle of twisted crumpled shapes.
Tangle of wreckage slowly disintegrates.
Death explodes, a pang of sadness.
Splinters of glass fly and scratch
tyres with punctures, hisses and skids.
Metal grinds, bending and crunching.
Crumpled body imprisoned in fumes.
A fire breaks out from a dented car.
Flames lick and roar
around ruins of blackening cars.
The siren of a fire engine blares.
Water sprays at the roaring flames.
They weaken and helplessly,
suddenly die.
Ambulances speed to hospital.
The remains are silent.
A thick smoke rises.
All that is left are the crumpled shells.

This was Alice's first draft. Later it looked like this:

There's a muddle of twisted crumpled shapes.
A tangle of wreckage disintegrates.
Death explodes, a pang of sadness.
Splinters of glass fly and scratch.
There's tyres with punctures, hisses and skids.
Metal grinds, bending and crunching.
A crumpled body is imprisoned in fumes.
A fire breaks out from a dented car.
Flames lick and roar
around ruins of blackening cars.
The siren of a fire engine blares.
and soon water sprays at the roaring flames.
They weaken and helplessly,
suddenly die.
Ambulances speed to hospital.

The remains are silent.
A thick smoke rises.
All that is left
are the crumpled shells.

This poem is just signed LF:

Instant destruction,
a cracked collision,
a burnt mangled jumble,
a winded corpse,
a grinded shell,
an upset wife.
A loose limp car door,
a destroyed gear box.
A squashed steering wheel.
A brake that failed to work.

The children on the video (Brigida continues) move into composition, a word I never use. But are they composing, dance making? How can I identify this? I turn to the dance community, to their literature, to Mary Lowden's book about the primary child *Dancing to Learn*. There is no reference to composition except for a brief note in the glossary:

> Composition. The way the dance is put together to make a whole work. It includes putting together movements, phrases, ideas, dancers, and music.

I rewind the tape to the beginning of the composition. I watch Christopher yet again on the screen. He sits at the back cross-legged, looking at me, the teacher. Scott sits beside him mirror-reflecting his position. Christopher glances towards the camera. During the words 'it's the skid' he rocks and lies back bringing his knees to his chest. As the music plays into the skid he opens out, rolls onto his left side, hands weaving in and out of the space in front, opening and closing his fingers. As the glass shatters his arms close over his ears and he seems to curve the upper part of his body which then becomes blocked by Scott's motionless, attentive pose.

This was a sequence of movements almost hidden, on the day it was filmed, but we found it on the video tape among sitting, listening children: ideas being tried out, put together into movements. They might be notes, sketches in a different art.

Just under five minutes into this part of the lesson, after continual teacher talk, I say 'Which way are you going to move with speed, which way are you going to skid, which way are you going to crash?' There's a demonstration from Sara that shows that when the glass shatters the movement keeps going with it. With the moving into groups I find Christopher on the screen. He works alone. At one point he sits and watches the others at work. I rewind the tape and watch every time he moves into the screen, slowing down his movements, and noting them.

He is ready, holds himself still, back to the camera. His left arm is diagonally across his chest, his right arm is behind, slightly lowered. As the car sound speeds through the hall he spins and spins across the floor out of the camera frame. In the sliding skid he leaps upwards and back into vision, but only just. His arms are fully outstretched, his head downward. He lands on his left leg first, the whole of his body tumbling to lie on that side. As he rolls onto his front the camera eye catches his feet, which are pointed, soles facing upwards.

When the children show their work again Christopher's sequence is almost an exact copy. Then he changes it slightly, lengthening it as he decides to move in the second and last crash rather than on the first. He introduces a crouched shape which may have its roots in 'As the glass shatters', he brings his arms over his ears and seems to curve the upper part of his body.

Both these movements suggest protection. His finishing position is the same. In both these sequences he spins across the floor, leaps to fall, rolls and rests, his body long. He is seen to be in composition, putting together movements, phrases and ideas stimulated from the topic of the classroom and the music of the lesson.

That is my interpretation of Christopher – but I want to know how he interprets this section.

I said to Fred later: 'I'd taught him dance briefly when he was six. He'd always done a lot of spinning, rolling, with his hands like this [on his groin]. He's still doing it. He used to sing oddly, hymns in the hall, eyes closed as if entranced, his voice going higher and higher, and the other children would look at him and laugh, but it was as if he didn't care. Later he was often in trouble: wild angry behaviour. I don't think we've ever released him. It's all been about writing, there's other ways for Christopher to find himself.

'Maybe his failures are our fault more than we like to admit, and if we are going to push children increasingly to pencil and paper for their expression, it'll only get worse for people like Christopher. If we don't release him, and others like him – but also unlike him! – we are building up trouble for ourselves, our society. And then, sure as anything, we'll know society exists!'

We agreed to meet after his packed lunch. It was wet and I found him playing marbles with a group of other children in the classroom. I thought he might want to stay with them but he came, set up the tape recorder and settled himself into a chair. I sat beside him. We watched him silently at dance making. I rewound the tape and we watched it through again.

'I'm going to play that little bit, the crash, again,' I said to him as I pressed the rewind button on the remote control to find the moments of his sharing, his dancing; 'and I wonder if you could describe yourself and the way in which you move. I'll play it as many times as you like.'

'Miss, he focuses on me all the time in that bit.'

'How would you describe your movements?'

'I don't know.'

But I wait, playing and replaying the brief sequence, my fingers moving swiftly from button to button.

'Miss, you've still got it on recording.'

'That doesn't matter.'

I still wait. His image flicks across the screen again and again. The silence grows.

'I don't really know what to say about it.'

'Can you describe how you're moving?'

We watched the sequence again.

'I get my curves in.'

'Anything else?'

'I don't know.'

'Can you remember what it felt like to be doing that in a dance lesson?'

'Painful.'

'Painful? Why was it painful?'

'Because when I did that . . .' (he pointed to the screen and I pushed the pause button).

'When you fell to the floor?'

'When I went bang.'

'How else did it feel?'

'Fast.'

'Anything else?'

Our brief dialogue ended. Silence. We watched the screen seeing time and time again the same, familiar movements.

'Strong ... like a wrecked body.'

'Is that what you were trying to do?'

'Yes. It looks like glass and bits of metal sticking out of me.'

'What I'm going to do this time is to put you into slow motion. Watch this.'

He leant forward in the chair, laughed quietly and watched as his movements began to slowly form before him.

'I was looking at myself and all those bits of lines are in the way.'

He's right. The lines, the noise bars, technical problems caused by the slowing down hid him, but I keep the theme going.

'Can you remember what you were thinking about in that?'

'Just being in a crash.'

'Were there any words going through your mind?'

'No, not really. Only the music.'

The interview in the dark television room was an uncomfortable twenty-five minutes. During the talk I became aware of Christopher's isolation, his vulnerability. He can't cope with one-to-one conversations. It was a cruel thing I did. The darkness separated us and the experience seemed cold. Words were pulled out of him through questions and long silences, forcing a response.

He is honest. 'I don't know. I don't really know what to say about it.' I didn't enjoy it and I wondered about him. But in this time Christopher described his movements in words and phrases that I, in my interpretation, hadn't seen or used. The pain felt through his fall to the ground in the crash, his 'strong ... like a wrecked body' that 'looks like glass and bits of metal sticking out of me'; the music igniting his mind into movement through his body.

FS comments: The lesson we learn from this is not that Brigida shouldn't have interviewed Christopher in this way, notwithstanding her guilt; but rather that such interviews, probably with more than one child at a time, should be an ordinary part of every school day. Through this kind of conversation children learn confidence and the vocabulary of an art, whether it is dance, painting, drama or a language art. So many writers have pointed out how little group work actually happens in classrooms arranged in groups: mostly children are facing each other, .but getting on with their own jobs.

But children could negotiate means with each other by talking in this way. They could, for example, be asked, in a group of four, to produce a report on a dance lesson. Each of them might concentrate on a different aspect of the work. This would enable them to use the language of dance to some purpose; it would work against the dreadful silences of Christopher's responses when he was suddenly pushed into the prison cell containing a video screen and a teacher.

Brigida writes: Another session with the video shows the children putting together movements and ideas. They have worked out who is moving where and when, for how long, and how that period of time is given order with movements and pauses. The sequences, although brief, have a beginning and an end, the contents of which vary both in movement choice and precision. Some are danced with confidence, with exactness, others are blurred, unsure and hesitant.

I asked Vicky and Amy: 'Would you like more time for dance?' and both children said yes. Vicky needed more time 'to do a lot better . . . to make up quite a good routine to show in front of people. Our parents teach us to talk and to read and to walk, why don't they teach us to dance?' Amy needed more time to 'get warmed up [and] get used to dancing. As soon as I'm warmed up and I'm ready to dance in front of people it's time to go out of the hall.'

I watch these two children in their dance making and their movements echo their words. There is a sense of uncertainty, a lack of flow and a disjointedness. This lack of time for them to explore and refine their ideas may derive from the continual input by the teacher, the constant intruding with instructions and ideas, and the lack of time for dialogue between each other.

How often do the children need more time to 'make up quite a good routine' not only in dance, but in science, maths, and painting. Making up 'quite a good routine' involves opportunities to redraft, discard movements, line, pattern; to rub out and begin again through dialogue, interaction and thought.

The arts suffer from this *curriculum interruptus*. Progressive primary schools are now out of fashion (though they were never in it). But such as there were have always, with their integrated day, been able to allow the child involved in some long term activity to get a good run at it. They allowed children to move through two or three drafts in a poem, for example; to play and experiment with colours or form. First school teachers have frequently lamented the accelerated change to periods of an hour each, when the children have to move to middle schools; from writing (three quarters of an hour) to maths (three quarters of an hour) to science (ninety minutes) – 'because it's time'.

The dance adviser talks of

> ... really talking and evaluating what they see, so actually taking the time to look and see; and not just say 'Oh, that was nice. I like that,' but 'Why did you like that?' [She talks of them being able to describe a movement in detail] 'I like that because the way Johnny picked up his foot he ... it was a delicate way, the strong way or the light way, or the forceful way, that he then added *that* movement to *that* movement'.

It was Christopher who brought the sharing part of the dance lesson into the talk with his group.

'Most people in dance, like if Miss Martino says, if you say, "Who wants to show?" most people don't do it, it's just the same people over and over again.'

'Why do you think that is?' I asked.

'Because they're like Nicola.'

'Do you want to say anything about that, Nicola?'

No response.

'Amy?'

'Because we might think we're rubbish at dance.'

'What is rubbish at dance then?'

'When you might make a fool of yourself in front of all your friends.'

'How do you make a fool of yourself? Amy?'

'Well, sometimes you say "you should have turned on that piece".'

'Do you want to say anything else about dance?

'Some people might think that they're not, they can't move in time to the music. The music might lead them astray and then they'll do a sort of dance but not to the music.'

'You feel stupid if you do something wrong like the piece that you wanted to do.'

'So what you've got in your mind isn't always what comes out through your body?'

'No.'

Sharing is part of the school day. The children's work is seen and celebrated, pinned to the walls, applauded through assemblies, shared in quiet moments between teacher and child, child and child. So why is it that, when it comes to dance, some of the children 'don't do it' and are worried about making fools of themselves? The more 'the same people over and over again' share, the more the gap widens between those that do and those that don't. Amy talked of 'showing myself to the class because of all the mistakes I make in dance I want to keep them secret'. This may well ring a bell with Fred who didn't want to share his feelings in the dance course in 1968, and who, it turned out, had good reason for his nervousness.

Amy's leaving the television room when watching the video, complaining of a headache, begins to make sense now, much as Fred's hiding behind his notebook does. But where does the discomfort and the insecurity come from? Is it the teacher not giving enough support or direction through lack of knowledge? Is it that dance hasn't been part of their past timetables and therefore hasn't been given a value until now? Is it a question about what is acceptable and what is not acceptable?

Is it the nature of the subject that brings with it not only a change of clothing to lighter garments and a revealing of body shape and size, but a response that is about sharing the private self with others: exposing vulnerability, nakedness? Without, as Fred has said in the previous chapter, any tools at all.

I asked the adviser: 'So what happens when a child is not happy about sharing even with a small group?'

> I think it's how you market it to them. If you make a big thing about it ... it is so difficult, isn't it?, because it is dependent on the personal relationship. But someone who is working with them all the time has a very special relationship with that group. I would start really small. Get the children, encourage them. 'That was really nice Johnny. I really liked that.' So you're actually giving that person confidence about themselves. 'Maybe you could just share that with us again.' Or it may simply be just that you are passing it round and that each person contributes something, and they have that moment where they have to and then you build it up gradually.

It is sometimes enough to give the child the confidence to share dance work either in a small way or through a sustained piece. But the teacher has to move other children towards sharing, because they are reluctant and, as the adviser said, 'the art form can't exist unless you share it'.

A work of art that isn't shared is a word in the desert. It doesn't even exist. The observer of a work of art – listener, looker, reader, whatever – is complicit in the act of artistic creation. He or she brings to the art act an interpretation that becomes part of the art. Indeed, an unshared art-act isn't only a word in the desert. It's a plane crashing in the desert because the pilot has died. Nobody hears the crash, because there are no ear drums for the soundwaves to hit.

Dance is a way of sharing the way we respond to the world, paying attention to experiences that can be organised in bodily movements. As in art, the child is involved with sensing and perceiving, feeling, creating and communicating. As in art, the child is involved with shaping space, giving it life through line and colour, the mind and body thinking, feeling. Christopher's brief sequence involved all these, not only in that moment but during the lesson as he worked towards structuring those movements. It is present in his words, in his body in motion, in his body in stillness as he tells of his experience of speed, skid, crash, death.

But sharing could also be brought by picture, video or visiting dancer. Dance in its many forms is a community activity and is not just for this group of children on a Wednesday morning with this teacher. It exists outside the hall, has always been and is present to draw on. If the children's experience of looking and seeing is extended through the community and becomes less insular, their understanding of dance would increase.

Christopher's talk came when the words were pulled out of him through questions and long silences that waited and forced a response. He was honest. 'I don't know ... I don't really know what to say about it.' Although he does describe himself in movement, a full appreciation of his experience is not yet, for him, possible. He doesn't seem to have a vocabulary, a vocabulary drawn from experience 'of really talking, taking the time to look and see, being able to describe a movement in quite a lot of detail' as the adviser put it. If more time were given to teaching the language of dance, to finding time to let the children practise it in groups, a vocabulary would emerge, just as it does with science, maths and other areas of the curriculum.

When sharing, the children become performers. The activity becomes aesthetic: that is, open to criticism, open to generalisation. Aesthetics is the science of the conditions of sensory perception. Whether dance is always working towards a performance or not, for the primary child it has to be aimed at a sharing: in the National Curriculum, participation and performance are key elements. An assessment of the performance is central. But how can those qualities that make dance an art be assessed? When I hear Scott's words:

What I wanted to do was to fall over and then roll into it, until it finished, but when I saw myself on video I really mucked it up and I thought 'Oh no.'

and Rebecca's:

You feel stupid if you do something wrong like the piece that you wanted to do.

I become aware that the art form is also held in the mind and that it doesn't always express itself through the body in the way that the creator may wish. It simply isn't open to measurement. Are the children to be assessed on what is seen, or on their thoughts and ideas, which they often failed to translate into movement? If the assessment is purely behaviourist, it will miss most of the critical elements. It will, of course, make a passable fist of evaluating technique, but will miss expression altogether. And it will miss the reasoning, often very complex, in the child's head, that leads, unfortunately, to no satisfactory outcome.

Sue Harrison in 'Assessment in Dance', a paper given at the Fourth International Conference in 1988 *Young People Dancing*, teases out what the content of a dance curriculum could be and how that could be assessed. She puts forward a number of points for those thrown into the assessment arena unprepared.

1. The assessment model chosen should reflect the style and teaching methods of the teachers involved.
2. The criteria for assessment should be laid out clearly; knowledge of what is appropriate and what is less appropriate is important.

3. The unusual or unexpected response should be allowed for.
4. The whole assessment should take account of process as well as product and context.
5. Creating artificial conditions for assessment should be avoided.
6. A variety cf approaches and conditions should be used for assessing the same thing.
7. We should look for a second opinion from other members of staff.
8. We should encourage self-assessment through developing motivation and self-awareness ...
9. ...and maximise feedback to the children through counselling, discussion and profiling ...
10. ...and ensure that future teaching situations allow students time to put some of their new knowledge to use, or time for remedial action to take place.
11. All assessment should be carried out with the utmost sensitivity.

Dance struggles for existence in a single attainment target in physical education for ages 5 to 16. It is hardly visible. Section 10 of Assessment in Physical Education states: 'The National Curriculum provides the opportunity to establish a national framework for assessment in physical education that focuses on what each child independently knows, understands, and can do'. With its emphasis on physical education it stresses 'accuracy, efficiency, consistency, adaptability, good line/design, effective expression'.

There seems to be a tension between the dance community and the demands of the National Curriculum, not only with the significance and value of dance on the timetable but the assessment of it. But there are links. Both look for expression, imaginative performance, expressing delight and pleasure in a performance, and talking about that performance, thinking of the aesthetic when making judgement.

But to whom does the teacher turn for guidance in assessment? A community with its love, recognition, understanding, and continual dialogue with itself about dance – or a legal document that locks an expressive art into physical education?

CHAPTER 7

Drama's Magic Box

In John Beynon's funny, vivid and moving essay 'Ms Floral mends her ways: a case study of the micro-politics of creative drama' (in Les Tickle's 1987 book already referred to), the head speaks for a million teacher-philistines around the world and down the centuries when, in assembly, he authorises the school secretary to collect dinner money during drama so as 'not to lose valuable teaching time elsewhere'. And three boys speak for millions of children when they comment that drama isn't going to get them jobs, that it isn't factual. 'Drama's buggering around, really, useless.' So drama has a low status, even among the arts: 'At least poetry helps you improve your use of language,' one girl said to me.

Like books and articles about dance and, to a lesser extent, the other arts, twentieth-century writing about drama in education is bedevilled by the polarisation between process and product. In drama, we might represent this gap in a particular way: it is between self-expression on the one hand, and theatre arts on the other. An extreme and vivid statement of the self-expression point of view comes from Brian Way, who distinguishes in his 1968 book between theatre, which is mostly about communication and audience; and drama, which is mostly about the experience of the participants. And he is concerned with the experiences of the participants.

On the other hand, Christopher Havell, working with Way's methods, and influenced by this 'highly developed and systematic methodology', remembers having difficulty in determining when the process was 'complete'. Against him one might argue with Valery that no art 'is ever finished, only abandoned'.

Indeed this dilemma need not concern us too much today, because all good work in primary schools contains elements of learning about oneself, and about performance. But the extreme 'self-expression' end is disappearing; performance is now most creatively represented by a group of children presenting their learning in dramatic terms to the rest of the class, to other classes, to parents – and not so often now in the huge and usually sterile context of the school play, where there is no necessary conversation between performers and audience. Drama in this book's term is a learning experience at least in part because it allows this conversation, this negotiation of social meanings.

To a generation of boys brought up in grammar and (I suspect) private schools in the fifties, drama is *Hamlet* with the school's star actor in the name part; a clever boy, but without Hamlet's looks, as Claudius; an up-and-coming boy as Laertes. The next generation still had unbroken voices – so its leading lights played Ophelia and Gertrude. (Real example: Henry Thornton School, South London, circa 1960. Hamlet was in fact played by Hywel Bennett, Gertrude by my little brother. The following year, he reminds me, his voice was on the cusp of unbroken/broken, so he played Flute the bellows mender in *A Midsummer Night's Dream*, the one who has to mimic a female voice.)

The same is true for girls: Mary Jane Drummond, who was at a convent school, has written in a letter:

I did drama too. The star actress was Antony, the naughtiest girl was Brutus, the cleverest Cassius, the prospective head girl was Caesar.

What was the effect of all this on Hywel Bennett and the star actress? We can make a few guesses. And what was the effect on the spotty youths of either sex chosen to be spear carriers year after year?

Sandra Redsell is an Unattached Teacher for Creative Subjects in Suffolk, working these days almost entirely in drama and dance. One should resist the temptation to see her peculiar title as some kind of commentary on how the arts are viewed in her authority: I am assured that there are no *attached* teachers for *uncreative* subjects. She also works at the Seagull Theatre in Lowestoft as a producer. When I met her she was producing *The Threepenny Opera*. We had worked together before, with a group of schools, putting together an arts week. She and I share a favourite theme, the magic box. I've derived a poetry lesson from Kit Wright's poem of that title in his collection for children *Cat Among the Pigeons*, and so have many other writers working with children: you put a box in the children's head, and get them to design it: it's your favourite colours, materials, size etc; it's got your most precious object in it, some impossible things, some worries that you can do what you like with. This poem was written by eleven-year-old Vicky:

My box is gold with silver lining.
It's got blue and purple alternative sequins around the edge.
It's got my initials on it in bold red letters.
It's got a little porky soft pig with big round eyes.
It's got a little ivy necklace.
Happiness is what the box is made of.
Fun and wishes spring out.
Out comes a tiny gold bell, ringing in the air
With two white faced dolls in pink frilly dresses.
A bright red unicorn leaps out.
Out emerged a purple ostrich swooping into the room.
Out jumps Louis Pasteur gulping down three pints of pasteurised milk.
Out comes the world sliding down a rainbow.
The box of happiness is closed and stillness is here.

This idea forces the children to compose an extended metaphor for themselves. It also offers opportunities for them to write sentences no one in the history of the human race has written before: for example, the one about Louis Pasteur. Another girl wrote: 'In my box/is the first note played by Mozart'. It turned out she was an accomplished pianist. This originality must be a central criterion by which we judge any work of art.

Sandra gave me a page of notes about her magic box lesson:

> I divide the class into small groups, then give out blank pieces of paper and ask them to draw either something they would like to find in a box or something they would hate to find. The size of the box would be determined by what is in it.
>
> We then collect all the contents together and just list them on the blackboard. I look for – and I encourage the class to look for – common or linking elements between the items. Sometimes it is obvious, sometimes it's difficult to see any common ground.
>
> We then begin to create a whole class drama from the given ideas ... I find it often a very revealing way into drama, you naturally get a lot of information about what the class is

interested in, but on both a factual and an abstract level: fear, hopes, excitements, past experiences, desire for adventure ... all those are often contained within the concrete object once we begin to examine the list on the blackboard.

I often take on a story-telling role, which can be taxing, but which is my control mechanism, and it's interesting how rarely the class bothers about the mechanics of including every single item on the list in the story once the concentration is really centred on the 'now' moments of the drama ...'

Today (9 December 1991) I watched her teach a drama lesson. 'It's not pure drama,' she says. 'It's a history through drama.' We were in an old-fashioned school hall on a cold, misty, dull day: tall stage, ineffective heaters making plenty of noise but no perceptible heat, a huge templated painting of a Viking ship on the back wall, the wintery backdrop for the school play on the front.

Sandra showed me her fingers. She'd already done one session in the hall when I arrived. They were blue and stiff, and she wrapped them round her cup of instant in the staffroom: 'It's bloody freezing in there ...' I asked her if there were any other requirements she had, apart from central heating; for example, the presence of the class teacher.

'As a visiting teacher you are at the mercy of the school, its policies, attitudes and schedules. I can't demand that class teachers remain with their classes when I teach, but in the main they do tend to stay in the lesson, although occasionally someone will say "Do you mind if I slip off to do a bit of paperwork?"'

'Well, I can't see how the teacher can either follow up or be involved with their class's work if they aren't present to see what's happening and I do sometimes wonder if they would skip off if it was a science lesson. Maybe that's an arts teacher's paranoia. But the basic point is that it's so very useful and revealing to observe your children without the responsibility of conducting the lesson yourself, it's one of the best forms of INSET. We can all learn from each other whatever the subject being taught, but I have particular sympathy for the teacher who is required to teach drama, has no training in it, has no idea how to conduct a drama lesson, and then gets sent off to do something else when I come in to work with his or her class – which has been known to happen.'

My Box

My box is a dark blue racing car shape.
Big as a house.
Made from sparkling polished diamonds.
To open my box, you slide the roof of the
car back onto the spoiler.
Inside is my mother who is kind and gentle
My father who may be away a lot of the
time but he really cares about me.
Also in my box is a rough caveman taming
a huge dinosaur in North America.
The first rays of light from the sun shining
on the universe.
A sheik's silver sword from Saudi Arabia.
A bald bat's beak from Budapest.
and lightning striking a man leaping
on me out of darkness.

by David Eaton
Age 10

Later in the pub we were to agree pessimistically – and a fraction self-righteously – that this was representative of a typical attitude to the arts. I had recently worked as a poet with a group of children, and one teacher, the head, had written his headteacher's report for the governors' meeting on a wordprocessor while the children were working. I'd assumed that the machine had been provided for the children to work on. The other had said to me: 'Will you excuse me for twenty minutes? I've got to get some petrol in the car'. Doing admin, slipping out of the classroom to oil the wheels of a real life – these actions teach children just as much, if not more, as the artist working for his or her art. They teach a belief that in the end the arts come after everything else: reports, science, sorting the car out. They don't really matter, not when real life is to be lived.

Children were lining up at the door, seeping into the hall. Whenever I'm in this situation as a teacher of poetry, I'm worried: you know none of these people, they are complete strangers, and in a little while – an hour, a day – they've got to have written notes for a poem, or maybe two; good poems, something that's better than their teacher could have achieved. Otherwise you'll have no credibility. I felt for Sandra and wondered if her lesson would ever get started.

Eventually 27 Y6 youngsters sat in the middle of the hall, where Sandra had placed a chair. The teacher and I set up camp at opposite sides of the hall. 'I want to take a photograph called "Christmas". What would it look like? Can someone show me? Put yourself in the photograph.' She blew on her knuckles and looked around the group with a powerful and persuasive optimism.

A boy puts his hand up. Sandra points at him – but it quickly emerges that he has no idea to offer. As soon as she points at him, he goes demure. 'Ah. Er.' (Finger vertically on chin and top front teeth, looks away, mostly at the door) 'Er ... Forgotten.' 'Do you want to have a think about it?' (Gratefully) 'Yeah.' Sits down. This boy has been in every class I've ever taught, not always a boy, of course; but there: believing that his enthusiastic smile and hand-waving will win him enough credit to get him past what emerges as his nothing-to-declare gestures moments later.

The second raised hand produces a success: another boy

gets two chairs and lies on his back on them, eyes closed, face expressionless. Sandra invites other children to join in the photograph. Girls come out, and stand behind the boy lying on the chairs. 'Where are you eyes looking? It makes a difference,' says Sandra, and the rest of the participants in the photograph look at the boy lying on the chairs. Or, more precisely, at his face. This is an exercise (like any genuinely artistic exercise) where there is no right or wrong answer. If she moves a child, it is only so the rest of the class can see him. More children come out and kneel in front of the reclining boy, or stand behind him, arms raised, beatific expression on faces.

'Well?' She questions the rest of the class. 'Well ... we think ...' (she says to the photograph) 'we *think* this is the baby Jesus, this is Mary, this is Joseph.' There's lots of touching as she teaches: hands on shoulders, encouragement to move with fingers under an elbow. Then she asks for another photograph: Summer.

One girl lies down on a beach, though it's the same chairs, happy expression on her face. Another sits on the floor, relaxing, eyes closed. A boy drinks, a girl reads a newspaper. Suddenly, it looks bizarrely like 'Dejeuner sur l'herbe'. 'I'd better not get any nearer to the Manet' says Sandra afterwards 'or we'll get arrested.'

In the last session, which I'd missed while teaching poetry in another school, they'd acted an accident. One child had been a car, the other a pedestrian. The rest of the class had been passers-by. The two principals had collided, and the rest of the class had been asked what had happened. Needless to say, the matter had come to court, even though the injuries had been minor. The accounts had differed greatly. On being told that the driver of the car had come from a pub, there'd been exclamations: 'Drunken driver!' and it was a matter of some time before the children had realised this might not have been the case. 'Maybe he worked in the pub ... Maybe he'd been drinking LA beer ...'

Interpretations of events were, of course, even more divergent than the accounts – insofar as 'interpretations' and 'accounts' can be separated. And that, of course, is the point. 'I am showing how there is no objective account,' said Sandra to me. 'How do we know what we know? I want them to understand how shaky word of mouth is. If this is true of a road accident that happened yesterday, how much truer it is of events from hundreds of years ago.'

I think of what I heard as a student: how the four gospels present differing accounts because of the evangelists' interests and obsessions – Luke the doctor and noticer of women's predicaments, John the Hellenic philosopher/theologian, Mark the journalist, always impatient ('And straightway . . .').

Now, changing from the summer photograph, they add to their road accident stories. They are inventive, attentive: so much of the National Curriculum is in use here. They 'speak', they 'listen' with great concentration to the other children, and to Sandra; they 'ask questions, and respond to questions, commenting appositely on what had been said'; they 'tell a story with a beginning, a middle and an end'. With great confidence, they assume their roles in play activity. (All these quotations are from NCC English AT1 Levels 2 and 3.)

Also, they are growing socially. The cliché is true: in drama, the least outgoing child will suddenly blossom. What one finds impossible in real life – say confronting a bully or a cheat – is practised in play. Later they will work with history, learning facts far more effectively than they would be if they were taking them from a book, or writing them out in tests.

'Freeze,' shouts Sandra, and they do. This serves two functions. One is aesthetic and educational: the children have to come to a still point, and they have an opportunity to look at and discuss each other's work. The other function is a control function. When Sandra wants quiet, the magic word achieves it instantly with no problem, probably because it is connected to the aesthetic/educational function.

Now Sandra looks at their freeze-frames. 'That's a great facial expression, faces are very important. Where are you looking? That's important too.' (Brigida in the dance lessons calls this a 'point of focus'.) 'This one definitely says accident, yes, lots of concern and worry . . . I can understand that' (she says to someone, who's spoken very quietly) 'I can understand that . . .'

Then she asks for a photograph from history. Her delivery is crisp and clear. She makes eye contact with each child, I'd guess, once every two or three minutes. Her hands are expressive, they flutter, they swoop, they aspire. And there are moments of stillness. When they stop moving, she is silent and so is the class. Teaching the arts brings about quietness. Get a class to draw an object close up, and their tongues go in their cheeks, or peep through their lips. They go quiet and sensitised. You'd think these moments were calculated, except that she's an 'actress', and technique and practice has made this sort of thing almost natural. It was Sandra who insisted 'actress' went in inverted commas.

'The reason is that I spent years trying to get certain headteachers to see that I was not an out of work actress but a fully trained, respectable teacher, just like any other, and even today some quarters will equate drama teaching with being a performer oneself – which is all right, except that the extension of that perception tends to be to see educational drama as frivolous and unnecessary.'

I asked Sandra about the theatre/drama debate that no chapter on this subject can miss out.

'Yes, we are working in a theatrical tradition ... we are using theatrical techniques, very disciplined drama techniques: role play, freeze-framing, mime. And yes, I think there may be performing elements in my work as a teacher. Perhaps drama teaching might reasonably be expected to attract people who either enjoy or have an unconscious alliance with performing skills ... though the possession of those skills is not essential to anyone wanting to either teach drama as a discrete subject or use it as a tool in the teaching of other subjects. Perhaps these performing skills, or elements of being an actor, are simply at their most obvious in the drama specialist since they are also the basic tools of control and communication employed by most experienced teachers. For instance, the way in which you use your voice – pitch, tone, volume, speed; facial expression – encouraging, puzzled, quelling even. There are questions of whether you sit or stand, your spatial relationship to an individual or the whole class – what does it say? Even the construction of a lesson could be seen as having theatrical overtones.

'But then of course teaching is an audience-participation experience, not a one-person show, and it's probably dangerous to extend the metaphor any further. As a drama teacher you are not giving a performance, you're trying to do the same job as any other teacher and your responsibilities to the class are exactly the same. The teachers who are entirely wrapped up in their own performances will achieve nothing of value with the children. But then, the qualities which individual teachers bring to their work is an aspect probably not given enough thought or respect either.'

I think that Sandra is right to be concerned with too strong a conflation of the actor/teacher role, first because it tends to devalue the teaching, and second because charisma, which must to a greater or lesser extent come with theatrical skills, is a controlling element. Many charismatic teachers do run highly successful 'one-person shows': entertaining – but educational? Not if we see children as active rather than passive learners; not if we define education in terms of negotiation and collaboration; not if we have learned the lessons of the sixties when writers like James Britton and Douglas Barnes pointed out that the talk experts in the classroom – the teachers – got nearly all the practice. The learners spoke the least. And this is the wrong way round.

In a charismatically theatrical classroom or drama hall, the same is likely to be the case: the children will get less practice than the teacher who is already something of an expert. Charismatic fluency is all too often a mode of control. Teaching dance, Brigida Martino is very concerned that her presentation shouldn't put other teachers off so that they can say: 'It's all right for *her* ... but not everyone can teach like that.'

Everyone can teach the arts, everyone, that is, with some understanding of what 'education' and 'aesthetic' mean; and teachers who let their powerful personalities get between the subject of the lesson and the pupils aren't doing anyone any favours.

All the lesson so far was a loosening exercise. Sandra is going to concentrate on history today. Her lesson notes say:

> The class will be encouraged to appreciate various simple aspects and methods which assist or hamper historical research; for example,
> - it's common knowledge,
> - we've been told,
> - we read it,
> - we saw it,
> - we look at surrounding evidence as well as what may be under your nose,

- we consider what may be surprisingly missing as well as what may be present.

The class will be introduced to the three main 'invaders and settlers' of the period 43 AD–1015 AD. Having been given written information about a certain common situation which might occur during these times, groups of children will be asked to interpret it visually. It is hoped that this method will give the children a sense of ownership of historical information.

Some statements of attainment which it is hoped might be visible in this lesson are:

- AT1 Knowledge and understanding of history:
  Give reasons for their own actions. L1
  Suggest why people in the past acted as they did. L2

- AT2 Interpretation of history:
  Distinguish between fact and a point of view. L3
  Demonstrate how historical interpretations depend on the selection of sources. L6

- AT3 The use of historical sources:
  Communicate information acquired from an historical source. L1
  Make deductions from historical sources. L2.

What is also visible here, of course, is the core study of KS2: 'Pupils should be taught about invaders and settlements ... the reasons for invasion (the search for land, trade and raw materials), the way of life of the settlers ...'

More importantly, it is hoped that the children will exercise the spirit of enquiry, desire for knowledge, processes of intelligent deduction necessary, not only for history work, but generally and in all their work.'

Sandra asks them to make three photographs: Anglo-Saxons at a feast, Roman doctors after a battle, and the construction of a Viking boat. The children, in five groups arranged around the hall, pose, argue, gather props: chairs, the piano stool, PE benches. Two girls near me turn a spit, cooking a deer. 'Do you really need two people?' asks a boy. 'Yeah, it's hard. . . . ' 'You shouldn't be moving, photographs don't move.'. 'I'm sawing her arm off. I don't care what happens to her! . . . '

They are pleasant rural middle class children. They live in a small town recently sent to doze by a by-pass that whizzes traffic from Ipswich to Lowestoft with minimal danger to places on the way. As they work in their five groups, the noise level is about right, apart from the odd squeal as a leg or arm hits the floor. I am reminded of the aim of almost all progressive teachers, whether they're teaching art, language, maths, science – or drama; a room where all the children are purposefully engaged on a task which they have, in part at least, designed themselves; where the teacher is not particularly visible to a visitor coming into the room, because she is at the level of the children, offering advice, asking questions, pushing them further: not, in other words, behind the altar, in obvious charismatic or priestly control.

The action takes about ten minutes. Then Sandra says: 'I'm going to count from 10 to zero. So you've got ten seconds to talk, to make it right. Then, when I get to nought, your photograph will be ready for us to look at.'

The whole class looks at and discusses each group. There is much talk here, but it is disciplined: you have to be to the point, because there isn't much time. The strategy builds the confidence of children who don't normally speak in a lesson at all. And the social learning is almost palpable, as they negotiate interpretations with each other.

Here is a group of doctors and amputees. Patiently Sandra draws from the class conversation about amputation, surgery, herbal remedies, anaesthetics, emetics:

'Is he praying.?

'No, I'm vomiting, I'm throwing up.'

The children are fully engaged. Occasionally a child comes up with an egregious anachronism: 'They're giving her an injection ... They're looking at a blood sample ... x-rays ... The Saxon chefs were putting meat in a concrete oven ...' When this happens Sandra makes them laugh with a wide-eyed look, and they realise their mistake. Even when they're right, she makes them think: 'So you've got a mast?' 'Yes.' 'Fine. And the mast? ... Where is it?'

There was a lovely moment as a shy girl worked on the side of the Viking ship. 'What are you doing?' 'I'm putting horsehair in the hole in the side.' 'What's that called?' Longish pause. Then a really *long* pause. Sandra lets it extend until it must be feeling like eternity to the child. Then the girl begins: 'Cau ...? caulking?' 'Yes, caulking!' To a boy: 'What are you doing with the planks?' 'They overlap.' 'So ...?' 'They are ... they are ... clinker-built?'

Later Sandra says to me: 'I suppose this is what critics of "modern methods" would call wacky, even uneducational, but the notion that the class is doing exactly what it likes without any teaching input is very unobservant. Just like any other teacher using these methods I have in fact researched long and hard the subject matter before I start the lesson. I'm trying to feed in information at the point when the class is most receptive to it, in other words when they have expressed, either through words or a "photograph" or a mime, their own perceptions of, for example, Saxon cooking or Roman medicine. We worked together for over an hour, covering an enormous amount of sheer factual information, if that's what's required. I bet if I'd lectured them on Viking ships, most of them would have been asleep after the first ten minutes.'

The children are given thirty more seconds to talk, to make their photograph better. Later she gathers the class around her. 'We're going to make a television news broadcast about an invasion by the Vikings. No, of course they didn't have television, but we'll cheat.' They listen carefully as she reads her script:

READER: Good evening. We bring you the news on this May evening 878 AD. King Alfred of Wessex and his army have taken up their positions in preparation for a battle tomorrow at Edington. We all know how terrifying the Vikings have been to us and we are hoping for a final battle to end all our troubles.

    You will remember how the Vikings, the Northmen from Norway and Denmark, have regularly invaded our country over many years. The first we know of them was when they destroyed the church and monastery at Lindisfarne in 792.

Here a group of eight or nine children make a photograph of the landing.

READER: Many people suffered terribly at the hands of these raiders.

Here two children make a 'film': a newscaster interviewing a woman – the shy caulker girl from the Viking ship a few minutes earlier. She avoids eye contact with the boy at first. He is much more confident. But gradually as she talks, she becomes more sure of herself, and she faces him and speaks up about her tribulations as a Saxon woman living somewhere on the east coast in the eighth century.

READER: Of course the Vikings saw things rather differently.

Someone puts the Viking point of view (presumably meeting the NCC point about understanding the invasions not merely as imperialistic ventures, but as desperate searches for land. This also attacks the idea of there being one perspective on anything.)

READER: Our quiet and settled Anglo-Saxon way of life is often interrupted by these raiders who simply want to take our people away for slaves, steal our possessions and then go back to their own country.

There's 'film' here of an Anglo-Saxon village.

READER: But now they want to settle here. They have not had it all their own way. In 876 as they tried to attack us from the south they lost 120 ships off the southern coast, at Wareham.

Photo of loss of ships.

Here time ran out, although Sandra had by no means got through her notes. We were suddenly conscious of the cold hall again, the fact that it was nearly lunchtime.

Later, in the pub, we mourned the anti-art stance of most schools. This is not entirely the school's fault. As I have noted in the chapter on Dale Devereux Barker's residency at Tattingstone School, the institution that is based on institutional values of conformity, safety and respect for authority will always clash to a greater or lesser extent with artistic values which, while they may be institutionalised too, will also remind us constantly of individual values. Art is Larkin's 'rough-tongued bell/ . . . whose individual sound/ Insists I too am individual . . .' and that individuality may be awkward, rebarbative and inimical to the institutionalised values of the school and the local education authority. And certainly it will conflict with the ultra-institutionalised ways of government.

Sandra said to me: 'Drama is not the best medium for communicating facts – names, dates, etc. Also it's not good for big battles, you know, like a Saxon raid, Boudicca's sacking of Colchester . . . It *might* be good for that. People think it is, children especially! But it will need a lot of planning, control mechanisms built in . . . it may be a recipe for disaster, the sort of lesson the original marauders may have appreciated.' Yes, I think. There's a poem somewhere, by Allan Ahlberg, about a class play on the Robin Hood theme that ends in the kind of disastrous scene Sandra is thinking of here.

Sandra offers the teacher follow-up suggestions: ' ... Each group is given an envelope containing, for example, pictures or notes relating to the home, farm, shop, they are to describe. Or Roman soldiers are returning to the Emperor and his advisers. Or Saxon/Viking raiders are returning to their families. Share each group's thoughts with the rest of the class, writing on the board with minimal comment.'

Sandra suggests rituals: 'Tell the class about the participants, the roles played, and the actions involved in an event which might lend itself to a ritualistic method of representation – mime, accompanying music/sounds, formal speeches, swearing oaths or declarations, use of special objects, processions ... work out in groups a ritualistic representation of a Roman wedding, a Saxon or Viking burial, a moot meeting, prayers and sacrifice for a sick Roman citizen at a temple.'

But isn't all this rather instrumental? What about drama in the purely aesthetic mode? The example I have shown here is of a given item in the middle school curriculum using drama as a reinforcing technique: reinforcing facts, attitudes, events, interpretations, attitudes; also increasing various skills: social, linguistic, movement, planning.

But does drama have a place of its own in the curriculum, as an aesthetic entity? Of course it does. Though if by aesthetic we mean that in some way drama can stand free of the rest of life, the answer must be no, unless we can conceive of an abstract drama in much the same sense as most music without words or action painting is abstract.

In the spring of the new year, I watched Sandra teach drama again. I met her at the Seagull Theatre. It had been recently decorated, and the woodwork at the front gleamed pink as sunburn. There is an auditorium, a studio, storage space full of flats and other theatrical paraphernalia, as well as teaching rooms and offices. There's a clean smell of fresh paint every-where, and old wooden-seated loos. The theatre is maintained by the Suffolk local educational authority, with smaller grants from other agencies like the Waveney District Council.

Appropriately, we talked about sponsorship. Sandra had heard about a businessman who had said sponsorship was marketing, and suggested that theatre companies negotiate with business before choosing what they put on. 'Eventually we'll have nothing but production after production of Oklahoma,' said Sandra. Certainly if business had had a grip of what was to be produced earlier this century, the experimental work of the modernists, say, would have been impossible. Musically we'll be reduced to repetitions of the 1812 Overture; our publishers will publish solely Jeffrey Archer, Pam Ayres and Frederick Forsyth *et al*, instead of only mostly so as at present.

Rory Kelsey is an advisory teacher for drama, and I asked him if he was aware of clashes between artistic values and institutional ones represented by the schools.

> Yes, there's the vest-and-knicks culture. Schools think you can't do drama unless you have a big stage, and the children always have to be properly dressed for it ... whereas we think you can do drama anywhere, and the children can be dressed how they like, though it often does help if they're changed ...
>
> I divided one class into groups and told them to talk about what they were going to do. The teacher was worried: 'But I won't know what they're saying!'

That was an extreme version of the distinction between the licence that art (so Poet Laureate Ted Hughes says) needs, and the control that schooling insists on.

As Sandra and I got lost in her car on our way to the school where she was to teach a class of nine-year-olds, she disagreed with me about big productions: 'Teachers don't like it when they put a lot of effort into a play and some clever dick comes along and says it's all ideologically wrong ... there's a lot of learning going in school productions, they're learning concrete skills, co-operation, they're learning what a production like that involves, they're learning internal discipline.'

They are learning their place too, I reflected sourly: beautiful people always in the big roles, the rest the extras, turning up rehearsal after rehearsal to say 'Yes my liege' or to sing the same lines of a chorus.

At the school, once headteacher Terry had explained carefully to the children what was going to happen on this drama course over the next few Friday afternoons, Sandra read the children the poem 'Making the Grade' by John Rice, from Gareth Owen's anthology *School's Out*. It's about failures, and ends with a daydream in which everything succeeds.

The children listen. They are obviously fully involved in understanding and empathising with the piece. One boy's eyes never leave her face. Sandra asks 'What makes him, or her, sad?' 'He wasn't good at anything ... he couldn't get in the choir ... he couldn't pass cycling proficiency ... he couldn't win any medals ... '. She accepts all these answers, often developing them, or helping the children to develop them, and then reads the poem again. The faces gaze. She reads, pauses, and they say the last line along with her.

She asks about the daydream the poet describes, and they answer correctly. But she adds to each answer. 'He dreams about scoring a goal,' says someone. 'Not just a goal, but the *winning* goal,' adds Sandra.

Then some of the children mime their daydreams. Michelle, who is later to play the role of maths teacher in the drama that Sandra designs, now plays tennis champion, up at the net, back, stretching her right arm across her body for a desperate backhand. Sam water skis, hopping on one leg with the other stretched our behind him, his hands stretched out in front, suddenly turning: 'I'm doing a fancy bit, I'm changing direction.' John casts off and removes a hook delicately from a fish's mouth. Christopher (in a Greenpeace tee-shirt) froghops around the front of the hall, k'slap, k'slap, k'slap, and it emerges he wants to be a grasshopper. Sandra, who always supports anyone whose answer might be in any way vulnerable, says 'Oh yes, it's lovely and free, isn't it, being a grasshopper.'

These little mimes, it occurs to me, are the basic units, the phonemes of drama. This is where it starts: in the moments when we think, what is it like to win at tennis, to water ski, to take a hook from a fish's mouth, to be a grasshopper, to be fierce, to be lost in a wood, to be out of work, to be a murderer, to be a charlatan, to be a very old person in a home, to be a jilted lover, to be a prince whose father has been poisoned, to sleep, perchance to dream? None of the things the children are doing looks like a play any more than piano practice at Grade One looks like someone playing a Beethoven sonata or a Brubeck solo; but this is the most important part, where the components of the vocabulary are being learnt. In these phonemes the children are practising for the rest of life. Much adult behaviour is, arguably, an attempt at going over again in actuality what has been gone over before – much more richly – in play or fantasy or fiction.

If this is going too far, it does forcefully suggest that play in all senses of the word is practice for adulthood; that what I have called these phonemes of drama are little ways into living an adult life that will add up to a kind of preparation. This is not to suggest that they aren't valuable for their own sake; but, conversely, it would be wrong to suggest that the arts don't have a preparatory value.

Sandra reads a second poem, 'New Boy' by Nigel Cox, about a first night at a boarding school. This offers a setting: she announces she is going to be the headteacher of a boarding school, and three children are going to be parents and a child coming to view the school. What will they want to know? How will the mum and dad be feeling? And the child? What will the headteacher want to tell the parents and the child?

Children volunteer, and at first are overawed by Sandra's intimidating headteacher. Then they ask questions, and Sandra asks them to freeze to show how they feel. In one example, Dad is extravagantly bored. Mum is sad, her head bowed. Daughter doesn't care. Another family react to the task differently: parents evidently can't wait to get rid of their son. He, though, shows distress.

Then Sandra finds another headteacher, an English teacher, a maths teacher (the tennis player, Michelle), a games teacher and a secretary, and sets them up at points on the outside of the hall. Two other class members are 'well-behaved children' (or 'best specimens' as Greenpeace Christopher puts it) who will show the prospective parents and pupils around. The rest of the class is divided into mothers, fathers and prospective pupils. They arrange themselves into families. While all this is going on, Michelle sits primly like a certain kind of maths teacher, as she sees it, unemotional and efficient, never dropping out of role. Michelle is clearly enjoying herself.

'Remember,' says Sandra, 'we are trying to find out about how people feel about this. You've never been here, you don't know anything about the place, you want to know if you want your child to come here – or maybe you want to find out if you want to come here.'

The headteacher, Victoria, wears a lilac leotard and has crimped reddish hair. The top half of her is in role, but her feet jiggle excitedly as the first threesome approach her. They've been shown in by the best specimens, who've then gone off to introduce another threesome to the maths teacher, Michelle, on the other side of the hall.

'We have chip dinners every five weeks,' headteacher Victoria is saying as I approach with my notebook. None of the actors takes any notice of me as I scribble in my rough shorthand. 'On Wednesdays we have spaghetti bolognese ... if the children are disobedient we put them in the hall. They must not be disobedient. Any more questions? Oh, they have separate playgrounds, the oldest in one, the youngest in the other. Do not worry, this is a good school.'

She is peremptory and brusque as later she dismisses the worry about bullying that an actor playing mother has mentioned. 'We don't have much bullying. When we get a bully, we lecture all the children in the hall. When the child comes here we make them have friends. They sit in the hall and they have to shake hands with the person in front of them, with the person behind, and with the people at the side of them, both of them.' I wonder if this is innovative new thinking about this problem, or something that happens in this school. Or maybe her parents (no, grandparents more likely) are encounter groupies from the sixties.

'Hello,' she says to new parents 'What are you looking for?'

'Friendly nice children.'

'Well, Sean and Margaret [the specimens] are nice, aren't they? Craig will be okay here. Any other questions? What do we have for breakfast? Hm. What do we have for breakfast? How interesting. I've never been asked that before. That's quite funny. We can't supply expensive ones, you know. Oh no. Ask Sean and Margaret, the ones who showed you around. They'll tell you all about the breakfasts, I expect.'

Victoria keeps eye contact remorselessly with the parents. Her brows are high, and she controls each situation with a haughty, sophisticated headishness that I would have found very intimidating as a parent and useful as a headteacher. She thinks before she answers. At one point she breaks off, looks behind the parents. 'What's the matter?' says one. 'Oh nothing – just two of my best pupils spilling coffee over everywhere!' I looked. There was nothing to provoke this fiction. Victoria was simply entering the setting with improvisatory gusto.

The boy who was the secretary held enormous power in his imaginary school:

'Do they have to wear uniform?'

'Yes.'

'What sort, what colour?'

'Blue, blue and white.'

'Blue and white.'

'I don't like trainers. No trainers in this school. Any shoes at all, except trainers.'

This dialogue shows children repeating what someone has just said, to stall, to make time to think about what they might say next. They rarely get such an opportunity in settings where the teacher is always on hand to contaminate the learning with his or her certainties. Children need more of these moments than they get – to experiment with language, to negotiate their meanings for the world. They stumble, learn about language – there's no teacher to helpfully (but not really) fill the empty space.

Michelle, the maths teacher, shakes everyone's hand as they approach her. She puts her head on one side to express attention. 'How old are your children?' a parent asks. 'Six and eight'. Then she painstakingly explains everything. She shows them all the teachers. 'There are no bullies in this school ... we do adding, taking away, timesing, and sharing, you know, dividing. I do the same for all the children, but some I push along a bit, they gotta learn, but mostly altogether, mostly I teach them altogether.'

Michelle is learning, but so is any observant teacher. So this is how they see us. This is how we seem to them, teaching timesing, sharing, dividing. Getting pushed along. They gotta learn.

On the wall behind her, the sun shines brightly on a display of notes on lined paper: Attainment Target 3 Level 3, SCIENCE by Junior Friday Group. Clouds, stars and moons hang from the ceiling everywhere. Terry hasn't left the hall, as so many teachers do when drama teachers work with their classes: he sits, dressed for action, not pinstriped. He is making notes. 'His spirit is very present,' says Sandra later, 'and that is very useful – he can snuff out any silliness, and he shows that what I do is important.'

Sandra joins in when one of the teachers is unoccupied. Michelle is clearly very pleased when Sandra sits opposite her. She sits, head slightly on one side, maintaining eye contact with Sandra's powerful presence, answers clearly.

Afterwards Sandra gets them altogether. Two boys are sniggering and giggling at the back and Terry walks up behind them. They have been working in here for nearly ninety minutes, which is a long time. Almost all the children are fully involved in the discussion Sandra is leading, which goes some way to summing up, bringing things to a provisional conclusion.

'They did use a formal language,' she says later in the car. 'I was pleased ... it was good ... what did you think?' I was pleased too. As the children step briefly out of their intimately known role, they learn about what it is to be a human being from a different angle. They imagine being a teacher or a secretary or a parent, or a child about to be enrolled in a school very different from his own. In playing these roles, they learn, engaged with concepts that normally flit by the edges of their consciousness.

But what dubious order this account imposes upon what happened! How much I've missed out, as I wandered about the room! Much I dismissed as uninteresting – thus my concentration on the headteacher, who had so much to say. Isn't the beginning of art a messy affair, higgledy-piggledy, harum-scarum, as all those English rhymes suggest?

Later a school rings to book me in for some work with children. 'Could you do some drama with them?' asks the teacher. 'Yes, of course.' Then I scrabble through my Sandra notes to find something I can do that sets a group of unknown children free to explore their world in terms of acting. 'What impossible things are in your magic box?' I ask. Eleven-year-old Stuart writes:

... a Stradivarius,
and EMI recording contract
with my name on it
and a letter from Nigel Kennedy
asking me to do
a Lullaby of Birdland duet with him ...

I wonder how I'm going to turn that into drama.

CHAPTER 8

Travelling Light in the Britten Room

All art may, as somebody said, 'aspire to the condition of music'. This is because of its abstract qualities, its direct appeal without the intervention of a medium of communication used for other purposes. Colour and shape are nature as well as art; bodily movements are sport as well as dance; words are conversations and shopping lists and well as narrative and poetry.

But notes and scales are always music. However, any precedence that this superiority might imply in the curriculum would be misleading. I searched and searched for good practice for a case study before I found Roy Blunden and his staff and, even later, Philip Goulding and Di Brendish. How many times did I turn up at a school, to find it was the wrong day? 'I don't think Mr/Mrs/Ms is expecting you.'

Had I been researching science or technology or (even more certainly) management styles and systems, they would have found something going on for me to look at; someone to talk to with views and experiences. But with music, almost more than anything else, we can say without shame, 'I don't think there's anything going on at the moment. Sorry.'

As a reviewer said in the *Times Educational Supplement*, the subject has suffered from a cycle of neglect in this country. But because music (like the other arts) is a way of knowing things – things about your self, your materials and your world – it is a vital component in any 'broad and balanced curriculum' (to use a current buzz phrase).

One of music's problems has been that intelligence has been commonly associated with verbal and analytical skills. So meanings to do with an art as intransitive as music have been devalued. We play records while we get on with real life: eating, getting our hair cut, shopping; but we don't value

131

what the art has to offer of itself. It provides an atmosphere, a background. A new restaurant that aims at a touch of class plays opera on the looped tapes – and if you're there long enough, the aria you heard with the artichoke heart salad reappears with the ice cream and coffee.

This marginalisation is being worsened by the current pattern of educational legislation. Emphasis on competition will mean that the music that schools are public about will be music that's (in every sense of the word) 'presentable': what's nice for the parents when the mayor comes; what the choir will do pleasantly at Christmas in the Town Hall. It is music in a neat parcel with a ribbon.

I worked in a school which had a good reputation for music.The choir sang sweetly and, as far as I could judge, accurately. One teacher played the piano, and another conducted. The repertoire was mostly familiar from my own schooldays: The National Song Book has survived surprisingly well. It also included songs from modern musicals: Lloyd Webber, of course, and others who had followed him in his path, writing pop operettas about Old Testament heroes. There were termly auditions for places in the choir: no boys applied, and several girls who did were turned away. Their voices weren't good enough. In most schools, music is like games in this sense: the better you are at it, the more you get. The weaker you are the less you get. With learning to read, of course, it's the other way round.

Visiting teachers for cello, violin and brass arrived weekly, as well as an unofficial guitar teacher. The most musical children got a go at most of these activities. It was quite common for a child with a good ear to end up her (almost always 'her') career in the school moderately proficient in three instruments. Frequently this child was also immaculately behaved: one noticed that there must be a formerly unsuspected correlation between musical proficiency and socially adept behaviour. During assemblies, music was played, and a teacher told children about the composer. A key word was always 'famous': 'This is a famous rock guitarist called Eric Clapton ... this is a famous composer called Mozart ... John, will you sit still and *listen*.'

At Stanley Goodchild's school, Garth Hill (see *Management for Change: The Garth Hill Experience*, Goodchild and Peter Holly), brass band music was the only art mentioned. It was a managerially oriented school with public relations a priority, and music is the art that need offend no-one. When I was a member of a Christian youth club, Beethoven's symphonies were played as background music by the ministers during our socials. They may have been written in the grip of human creativity and sadness; or in triumph at what the human race could be; but they were used as inoffensive background in a way Shakespeare's Sonnets could never be.

And this isn't just because the sonnets are words, and we have to listen to words in a compulsive way we don't experience with music. Music is easily made background. This is because of that intransitivity of its language, and (as Auden put it) it is just that intransitivity which makes it meaningless for a listener to ask: 'Does the composer really mean what he says, or is he only pretending?' It is not at all meaningless for us to ask that question of a poet or a novelist or a painter. Those arts are actions that 'pass over to an object', to use a dictionary definition of 'transitive'. Music isn't like that.

Questions about truth, sincerity, honesty – and implicitly about ideology and politics – are relevant to the other arts, and make those arts that provoke them questionable in a school that values its image above everything. Brass band music avoids such tensions.

As we have seen, it is quite possible to disempower Dale Devereux Barker's work by selling it as upmarket wallpaper for some new office block in the Docklands; and to leave Schubert alternately aggressive and cajoling as I type this is equally disempowering. To limit music to the ablest, the beautiful people with good ears, voices and behaviour, is to disempower the other children. John Mills, a teacher in a special unit for children with learning difficulties, who often have deep emotional problems, believes that music can have a therapeutic effect; the less beautiful people need it more than the others.

But music is the art that has survived least well over the past few years. I rang music advisory teachers, primary advisers and many headteachers before I could find some practice that anyone would recommend as worthy of description in a book of this kind. The Plowden tradition has left many classrooms rich in the tradition of the visual arts. Alec Clegg and writers like him have ensured that imaginative writing thrives. Drama and dance are rare – but not so rare as the imaginative music teacher.

Music may be acceptable in a profit-obsessed society because, as I've said, it doesn't seriously risk offence. But it is only narrowly vocational, and that for a very small number of people. And it is expensive, and that is what is called today the bottom line. If sponsorship takes total control of performed music, orchestras like The City of Birmingham Symphony, under the internationally acclaimed Simon Rattle, will not get the work they want, as this cutting from *The Guardian* of 14 March 1992 shows:

> ... those in the arts are increasingly frustrated at being told to use their initiative to find more sponsors. You couldn't find a more enterprising orchestra than Simon Rattle's CBSO which has enlivened Birmingham no end, yet it has been unable to find one sponsor, however small, to finance a forthcoming tour of the States ... Instead, the orchestra has settled for a 14-day tour of the east coast in April. And it is only managing that because Mr Rattle and his soloists have agreed to forego most of their salaries.

As I write a furious debate is taking place. The Secretary of State wants a greater emphasis on the theory and history of music, which are much cheaper than practical work, while Simon Rattle and other prominent musicians are anxious that the best practical experience children get shouldn't be lost. The most eloquent defence of practical work comes from a journalist in *The Independent* who is learning to play the piano. He tells how trying to play a simple version of the opening of a Mozart symphony taught him more about Mozart than all the articles he'd read during the previous year.

Trying to instil respect for Mozart in young children by making them listen to the Jupiter symphony is like trying to make them into great dancers by watching videos of Fonteyn and Nureyev. It won't work. The best way to instil respect for music is to make sure they have the access to the materials with which they can make it.

The nine-year-old children are preparing for a performance in eleven days time at the Snape Concert Hall, Aldeburgh, scene of many Britten premieres and probably, London and Birmingham notwithstanding, a centre for musical excellence in the United Kingdom. There's also going to be some dance.

'We're performing it in front of some people,' Sarah and Christopher tell me, understating somewhat the setting. 'It's about four telephone calls, a sad one, a happy one, an angry one and a surprise one. The sad one's, well, not very happy. It has chime bars going doo-doo-doo [rising, C E flat G] slowly and the little xylophones going at the same speed and the triangles keep on tinging and the scraper goes scrrr scrrr scrrr, you know ... We made the music, we told him (teacher John Mills) and he wrote it down.' (see transcripts)

One of the children thought Sir had written the music. John resolved the problem: 'I supplied chime bars,' he wrote to me later, 'in a major key for "Happy" and a minor key for "Sad". Then the children experimented.'

He also let me have a tape of the music. 'Happy' is quite conventional with a guitar accompaniment keeping everything in order, and chime bars and indian bells on top playing a cheerful, simple tune, D A F sharp A. There are no drums or woodblocks. 'Sad' begins with a guiro, a scraping thing, and moves into the simple tune one of the children had already described to me. 'Anger' is, obviously, aggressive – two beats on a woodblock repeated several times, and a drum arriving late during a gradual crescendo. Then cymbals end it. 'Surprise' is all shakers with 'Woodblocks/small chimes like fast ticking clocks. Large chime bars up and down scale' as John's notes put it.

Christopher continues: 'I play in "Angry", it sounds like a load of rackets. I like to play one of the things with all metal balls on ... when I play "Angry", my hands hurt 'cos when I've got to play my instrument it's all the way through.'

Later there's a rehearsal in the hall. It's the first time (both the teachers tell me) the dance and the music have come together. 'It'll be a shambles,' says one, speaking for both, but also for every teacher everywhere faced with a stranger about to see their work when that work is about performance rather than process. 'The ones who've got sticks,' says Alison, the teacher responsible for the dance, 'they'll be wearing masks, Margaret [a colleague] and her class are making the masks ... they'll be rather stylised.' 'It has to be,' John says later, 'when it's a performance ... the emphasis has to be away from the process when you are putting on a show.'

Elsewhere I have noted that the product has to be important as a staying point for reflection on what has happened and what will happen: here it is very prominent in the teachers' minds – understandably, given the setting. There are twenty-one children. Eleven are stripped variously for dance: a few leotards, a few tee-shirts (Cheers! says one; and another, Sharp) and shorts. The others are in various forms of the school's dark blue and white, sweaters, shirts. A girl is sent to get a tape for me, runs back in, deferential, glad to be of use, cautious and meticulous. The children absently plonk on or shake their instruments, chatter until John silences them: 'There should be no noise from the musicians before a concert except tuning up, and that doesn't apply in your case.'

They'll do 'Happy' first. Alison had told me how some of the dancers had discussed and choreographed movements but that they'd returned to country dancing when asked to dance to music. I can see what she means: the happy music begins with four triangle noises; then paired notes (D A; F sharp A; D A; F sharp A etc) but somehow the dancers have contrived a country dance, arch and arched, to this.

John complains about the music: 'You've never done that before!' (about a mistake). The teachers talk to each other, the children wait. How many times have I participated in this situation? When there's a big product, a presentation at the end of a scroll of curriculum, is it inevitable? The teachers become more concerned about the big moment in public than they are about the learning the children are going through, and this inevitably questions whether performance is educational at all. They are slightly worried, and my presence isn't helping. I try not to feel guilty, and go on making my notes.

John says, 'I know, but I haven't had the time. Chime bars are very loud instruments, but they've got to be played loud ... some of it sounds like a British Rail train announcement.' Then he says, crouched, as if half-genuflecting, over the stereo equipment: 'Help! This isn't working!' When it does (Alison has sorted it out) it plays the same music, recorded by John. The children do the dance in the skip we are all familiar with from countless playground duties, from several Opie covers. It's a kind of template of childhood. Glockenspiels play the simple melody. On the tape, which I listen to in the car later, John's guitar holds it all together. A drum booms. They freeze.

'Now we'll do "Sad",' says John. 'They are very nervous,' Alison comments. It's slightly different from the tape. Scrapers,

Happy.

Key:
* indian bells
↓ large chime bars
↑ small chime bars
β bass xylophone.

Sad

Key:
- ⋀⋁ guiro
- △ triangle
- ○ tabor
- ↓ chime bar

NB The words are whispered by the chime bar players.

Anger

} — × 5

} × 12 (with drums and claves becoming more and less intense)

leading to followed by silence.

Key: I¹ₓ   large woodblock   cymbal

       I²ₓ   middle woodblock   ♂ drums

       I³ₓ   small woodblock

       △ triangles

       ♂ -claves

Surprise

♪♪♪ 🎵🎵 ♪♪♪ 🎵🎵 ♪♪♪ 🎵🎵

♪♪♪ 🎵🎵 ♪♪♪ 🎵🎵 ♪♪♪ 🎵🎵 } ×4
△△△△ △△△△ △△△△

continue rhythm whilst (freetime)

 Glissandos on glockenspiel
 Woodblocks / small chime bars like
    fast ticking clock
 Large chime bars up and down scale

All leading to crescendo after about

16 bars → (cymbal) → (vibroslap)

Key: ♪ Cabassa   (♪ ♪ ♪ 🎵🎵)
    🎵 Claves   (1 2 3 ×4)

    large cymbal

    △ triangles
    "Black Adder" (vibroslap).

drum, slower glockenspiels, tambourines shaken in a simple rhythm. When it comes to 'Anger', there's a Yesssss from the boys on the drums. John has high hopes here: 'They actually argue with the wood blocks.' I look at this section and they are all boys. The feet of the dancers, a different set, go in the rhythm of the wood blocks. Because the theme is anger, the dancers' focal points are each other's eyes: they glare, stare, threaten. This is very good, I think. Perhaps the 'Happy' dance wasn't as focused as this, literally. Drums come in later, threatening the wood block noises, that get louder. A cymbal ends it. 'The drummer is one of the people who couldn't come,' says John. It's all angular. There's a crescendo. A girl in the tee-shirt saying Cheers stops dramatically.

Then they play 'Surprise'. I can't help thinking, where's the phone conversation gone? Perhaps that's the surprise? Later, I spoke to four of the children about the project. They were sure there were telephone calls, and John said it was part of a communication topic, so there would be a telephone motif, but Alison said no, they probably wouldn't bother. I asked them what other music they do in the school.

'We all play recorders.'

'All of you?'

'Yes, everyone'. The teacher, Margaret, who makes a point of her lack of musicality, joins in. 'Oh yes, we all play recorders here, but we're pretty terrible'. They demonstrate: 'I'm going to count to four, I should count to two really, I'm going to count to four though, stop fussing, are you ready ...'

It's The Grand Old Duke of York, rather ragged. 'Where did you go wrong?' says Margaret. 'Other people did Ds Miss'. Then, much more together, Ten in a Bed, the little pale ringed fingers stretching to get up and down and round the instruments. Finally London's Burning, perfect. Massed recorders are the musical equivalent of Lambrusco, slightly fizzy in tone, thin, cheap sounding. Jonathan, who hasn't got a recorder, sings along in perfect tune.

I lead a second group to make it a round. 'Where will you bring yours in? On the first "Fire"?' Margaret asks me, as if I should know. But, slightly to my surprise, I do know when the moment comes, and we end up finishing the piece immaculately. And it sounds perfect again. We look happily at each other, the way people do who have made music together.

I ask a group of children what music they like: Symphony music (Simpson's music!? says someone, Jonathan I think). Disco music. Pop music. Classical music, any classical music! All sorts of music, but especially Queen (this was only a few weeks after the death of Freddie Mercury, so the revivals of his songs were flavour of the month). Jason. Kylie Minogue.

I asked them if music is as important as maths or English. Chris says, 'Nah. You don't really have to know about music ... if you don't like it you don't have to know about it. You have to know your tables, you have to be good in exams to get a job.' This seems to be a good encapsulation of government's vocational thinking about education. But Amy and Kirsty disagree: 'My dad,' says Amy, 'thinks music is important, he's got a CD player, a record player, lots of records, classical and Queen and all that music from Fantasia ... Music is as important as maths and English because if we didn't have music the world would be totally dumb. Music is as good as maths! You could get a music person job, a piano tuner, a piano player, a recorder player.'

Kirsty said she did ballroom dancing: 'And if you didn't have music you wouldn't be able to dance. I listen to my mum playing the piano, and I listen to waltzes. I like it when Mr Blunden plays his guitar in assembly. And when he tells us a story. He plays Chariots are Coming.'

Roy Blunden is one of those enviable headteachers who have an alternative to stories, poems and assembly collections for his morning stint before the whole school. He can, with two chords, get silence and attention and, probably, engagement. Why, I asked him, is music important? What does he think of the current debate: learning the heritage, or practising music?

> I would not want the impression to take hold that Cliff Lane is *the place* for creative music! We do it, but in a fragmentary sort of way, and each in a different way. As far as the work John and Alison did, I was the enabler, not the driving force. At Snape I will be a guide, a helper, a runner, etc (and, in parenthesis, a 'fan') and I suppose I will use all the old tricks to get the best from the children.
>
> Music, like maths, is either the thing you can do and enjoy enormously, and develop creatively; or you hate and avoid like mad, falling back on the specialist who 'does the singing' or 'does the maths scheme'. It is very hard to encourage the class teacher who fears music to give it a go.

The problem is implicit in the performance aspect, I think. When you have painted a picture or finished a graph you may still refine it, improve it, even hide it. But music depends on performance, like the children will be at Snape, and everybody knows (one feels) if it goes wrong, doesn't work and so on.

Music is a great bonding feature for a group or class – they have to be interdependent, they have to question, they will develop the music, etc. They also begin to realise that groups have to have dynamic and structure, just like the music they are creating: for example, someone in the group has to start the piece *and stop it*! I am a virtual non-musician, although I can sing a bit and know a few guitar chords. But even with a story-reading session with children I try to use some recorder music – often only to relate the music of an African country to an Ashanti story, or Bhangra music for the Rama/Sita story. And I will use creepy sounding 'classic' music to set the mood for a ghost story.

I do not feel in any way qualified to comment on the Music National Curriculum yet, but as with so much else in the rest of it, I find its ethnocentricity worrying and exclusive.

At Aldeburgh, a fortnight later the children chatter nervously. It's time for the big production. There's a poster on the wall backstage at the Snape Maltings concert hall:

A Celebration of Schools Music
9–14 March 1992
at Snape Concert Hall
7 pm each evening
During the week (it continues) over 1500 pupils from schools throughout Suffolk will 'Take to the Stage' at Snape Concert Hall. With a programme including orchestras and choirs, jazz groups, rock groups, dance, drama and classroom activities, this is a week not to be missed.
Presented by the Aldeburgh Foundation Education Department in Association with Suffolk County Council and sponsored by Kimberly-Clark, makers of Kleenex Products.

I'm carrying in my wallet a piece of headed notepaper signed by Roy Blunden that says:

To whom it may concern:
The bearer Mr F Sedgwick is a bona fide helper for this school's item on this evening's programme.

Signed ...
14 March 1992

I'm not really a helper at all. But four week ago, after a long intermittent search, I found a school taking music seriously. Not just music for the golden ones with nice voices and good ears, but music for everybody: and it was obvious I had to write about it. My worry was that I wouldn't get in, because the evening was a sell-out. Indeed, many of the parents, including the parents of Cliff Lane, were relegated to a hall where the concert was being relayed on closed-circuit television. And I am always worried about officialdom getting in my way. In fact, I had no trouble at all getting backstage. I passed young dinner-jacketed, or formally white-bloused, stewards, to find myself in a corridor full of school students of various ages chatting excitedly. Then, eventually, after asking a few people, the Britten room.

It's full of children in that indefinable state that means they're about to perform in front of their parents, but also in front of other adults too. They chatter, their voices raised. They point, laugh, make fun of each other. On the wall is a portrait of Britten by Dulcie Lambrick. He looks innocent and penetrating as he gazes out of the dark background. Two girls look at him gratefully from the edges of the canvas. There are other pictures all around the room: nothing that would give any offence, safe art 'stuff/Nobody minds or notices' (as Larkin puts it in 'Livings'). Not quite as extreme as that encapsulation of the genre as 'Fishing boats drawn up on the beach at Aldeburgh' and 'Poppies in the Corn near Snape' – but not far off it. Alison Smith, the dance teacher, is calming the children with poems and games. Later, we all take a turn in this job. I find I do know Charles Causley's poem 'Mary Mary Magdalene' off by heart after all, and I say it to them as quietly as I can.

At last, here is a production. We've seen finished poems and pictures, but in schools the emphasis is nearly always on the process, despite pressure – the testing movement, for example, and the target structure of the national curriculum – to spoil this. Most schools know that if you get the process right, the product will be right too. Here, on the other hand, the emphasis is firmly on a five-minute period at the end of it all: a little moment out of time, it will feel like to the children. They will, as Roy said, feel exposed. Then they will wonder afterwards where it suddenly went, once their teachers have left them in the charge of their parents, and gone to the pub for a pint of Adnams, or a glass of red wine; I'll be there too, writing this up. Maybe this strange fleeting moment, this climax, this having to be special, silent, not too quiet, not fazed by the lights and the atmosphere, perfect – maybe this moment out of time is educational in itself.

The children look different, in leotards or school uniform, as they chatter around the room. Only the teachers look the same, in casual clothes, black jeans, casual sweaters. They've had a rehearsal during the afternoon, and John Mills, the music teacher, tells me: 'It's a funny feeling being up there on that stage. They respond well, they stick to you, you're like a mother hen. And that's to the good, it has to be good, it has to be very well-rehearsed, so they can get the confidence it all needs. But they have to retain some spontaneity too. In another hour it'll be all over bar the shouting.

'For me music, poetry, all the arts are the stuff of life ... the rest of our efforts ultimately serve and service the arts. You watch the children in a minute – even holding the beater they're dancing.'

During the afternoon, the children had played in the grounds around the hall, clambering through the Hepworth statue which has no DO NOT TOUCH notices on it, and which therefore stands as a kind of symbol for the arts as I think they should be: open to everyone. The children interpreted this piece as all children do when they first see it; they climb through it, stand on it, crawl round it, hide behind it, coming to terms with it and the space around it physically as well as emotionally and intellectually.

Referring to some work in an earlier rehearsal, only ten days ago, John says, 'We've dropped the telephone motif ... we found we didn't really need it.'

It's seven o'clock now, and we're waiting to go on. Roy tells the children: 'You saved that little bit to make it special. You've been marvellous, but now you're going to find that extra. The audience is there, your mums and dads are in the video room, waiting to see you. Don't look at the lights! Use all the space. Enjoy it. Have a good time. Don't be afraid of it!' All the old tricks he calls this, but it looks like good encouraging humanity to me.

Roy tells me later, in the pub: 'They weren't selected, those kids, that's important ... or they were self-selected. If they wanted to do it, and they came to rehearsals, they're in it.'

None of the children admits to being nervous, but they bubble, and John plays a calming chord on his guitar. Then everyone sings a distantly familiar Cliff Richard song about not bothering with anything more than a toothbrush. The children do weird trans-atlantic accents, short flat a's and nasality, and sing with enthusiasm about hearts full of love and pockets full of dreams.

I pass the orchestra dressing room. It is empty except for chairs, instrument cases, clothes. Disembodied sounds drift from the hall, and I recognise the music: Vachel Lindsay's poem 'The Daniel Jazz' to a syncopated setting by somebody or other (Herbert Chappell?). A school choir from St Matthew's in Ipswich sounds to me as if it is doing a superb job of it. Here's a crescendo:

> And Gabriel chained the lions
> And Gabriel chained the lions
> And Gabriel chained the lions
> And Daniel. Got out of the den ...

In the corridor the Cliff Lane children shiver with nerves. One yawns hugely and at great length. Staff move massive equipment around silently. A child talks and is immediately shushed from five directions. The choir on stage go up an octave.

> And Gabriel chained the lions
> And Gabriel chained the lions
> And Gabriel chained the lions
> And Daniel. Got out of the den ...

Students holding scores whisper outside the hall door.

> And Darius said 'You're a Christian child ...'

Once the stage is cleared, the music adviser announces Cliff Lane, emphasising that these children have written their own music and choreographed their own dance ('This work comes from the classroom. It's all the children's work. They're years three and four or, in old money, first and second year juniors. Or in even older money, seven and eight-year-olds.')

The kids come on with John and Alison. I've found a place at the front of the auditorium, kneeling in front of the front row of chairs. I scribble in my notebook. 'Are you from the *East Anglian*?' a lady says, the steward, referring to the local daily paper.

A class has designed masks for the production. The dancers hold them on sticks in front of their faces. The 'Happy' music is first. It's still very country dance. The children – there is at least one boy in each dance group – skip around the stage to the cheerful music. The masks are yellow. The elderly ladies in the front row are charmed, their smiles fixed and sincere.

For 'Angry', the lights dim. The masks are orange. John conducts them, exhorting more volume, hands round ears. The rhythm instruments clatter and bang. The chime bar players mouth their notes as they play, their instruments sellotaped to the stage because they drifted around during the afternoon.

Blue masks: the 'Sad' dance. Alison is crouched behind the piano, trying to watch every movement. The silent choir of older children behind watches intently in the half dark.

'Surprise' is white, provokes laughter, and then it's over. The black adder, the vibra-slap, judders. The children leave the stage quietly. Back in the Britten room, Roy says 'That's the best you've ever done it ... Brilliant'. A girl says 'I wanna do it again'. 'Brilliant' I say to everyone who'll give me a second of their excitement. 'That was brilliant, Alison ... John ... Roy ... Clare ... James ...' The next school have their eyes on the stage, are making their way through the curtains.

By contrast, I saw some music at St Helen's CP also in Ipswich which aimed at no production. Entirely art for art's sake, I'm tempted to write, but it isn't true. There was nothing fey or decadent or unnecessary or limp about what these children were doing. It was art for education's sake, possibly, or even art for humanity's sake. It was art – music – as an essential part of growing up.

When I arrived, ten-year-old Antonia gave me a list of all the musical instruments available:

auto harp
clay drums
post horns
hand castanets
handbell
tin whistles
ocarinas
four shakers
two bass recorders
trebles
tenors
contra bass
psaltery

Later Di, the teacher, gave me another list, of 'basic instruments used by all classes ... the instruments that I had taken in were specifically for the group pattern. The children should have been using the school basic set for the rhythm, slow quick quick basic rhythm, but because I was screwed up by your being there I hadn't sorted that out, and the children didn't correct me. They should've had two sets of instruments, the ones you saw plus a selection of the more normal ones. I only realised when I read about the poor child blowing down the horn and trying to get the basic pattern from that, poor thing.' So Di was yet another teacher mugged into uncharacteristic error by a writer watching. The list of basic instruments was:

tambourines
triangles
claves
cymbals
drums
maracas
castanets
chime bars
wooden agogo⎫
cabasa afuche ⎪
vibraslap   ⎬Latin American instruments
mutti-guiro   ⎪
xylophones   ⎭
glockenspiels

There's a haze of music going on when I arrive in the hall where Antonia and the rest of Di Brendish's class are beginning their weekly music lesson. The classroom had been impressive in the evidence of variety and strength in the visual arts: sculptures made of wire, surgical bandage, cotton, wool, where (as Helen said to me) 'the spaces between things were as important as the things themselves.' There's also some batik around the room, in lively fresh colours and shapes.

The first five minutes in the hall are composed of a warm-up: perhaps all the arts need this loosening session before the substantive issue takes over in any lesson. Certainly Brigida and Sandra (in the dance and drama chapters respectively) work in this way. Then, of course, I suddenly realise: there's another way of looking at this. It's like a nursery where equipment is already out when the children arrive, so they can start to play/work immediately they arrive. There is no sterile silence, waiting for the magisterial presence of the teacher. The children are working from before the word go. There is no time wasted on administrative tasks like registers: we are here for music (the arrangements says) so we get on with it straightaway. The way a setting, whether classroom or hall, is arranged teaches children something. This setting teaches the children something about the centrality of the musical experience. The children play in six groups arranged around the hall. The one I've sat down with have Pan pipes, chanter, recorders and a polythene bottle that makes a good strong drum noise.

Then Di puts on a record, a traditional labyrinth dance called Pogonisioś, with a rhythm she spells out to them: 'slow, slow, quick, quick, slow'. ('I do Greek dancing myself and so I found it quite easy to bring that into my lesson'.) The children form a queue and dance, reversing in time, turning round, not at all like Victor Sylvester. They look like a Coke advert, a model of human harmony, because this class is a rich mixture of ethnic groups, and St Helen's is famous in the authority for its innovative work in multicultural education.

'Stop,' says Di. 'Now keep that rhythm in mind and go back to your groups and get that rhythm going on your instruments.' She claps her hands. 'Music is about counting, amongst many other things.' Then she changes the rhythm with the tambour, and children come out individually to show how to change the rhythm on their instruments. 'Good girl ... good boy ... well done ... You see what he did? You heard it? He kept the first note the same but lengthened the second one. Not "boom boom bom bom boom" but "boom bom bom boom boom'".

A Sikh boy does another variation on his Pan pipes. Joe's group, mine, has acquired two post horns, ocarinas and chime bars, and the five children play the rhythm with them. The post horn is incredibly difficult to get a note from, like a trumpet in that respect, but one of them manages it.

Sandy's group all have instruments that have strings, including a piano which is open, and a boy is making harpsichord-like noises with it. In another group, a boy stands holding a football, and I do a double take: is he going to be told off? No, it's a very solid rhythm instrument as he drops it on the floor, catches it, drops it again.

'Always make it really unusual,' says Di, and I'm surprised to note that this is the first time I've heard another teacher say anything to this effect. 'Make it new' is a motto for me (self-contradictory, true: Pound made it his mantra fifty-odd years ago, of course, and by now there ought to be a new way of saying it). Other versions of it are 'Make it yours' and 'Make it different'. Originality seems to be the indispensable condition of any artistic enterprise, and here Di is saying the same thing. I want sentences that no-one in the history of the human race has ever written before: yesterday a girl wrote, for example, 'a lie wearing pink bows can be believed'; and Di wants the same in music.

A child comes in the door with a message. 'No, I'm very very busy,' says Di. The child retreats, and I wonder what his teacher's response is going to be. Then, seconds later, a parent comes halfway into the hall: 'I want to see Sybelle. I want to leave the key for her.' There is an edgy moment as the mother talks to her daughter, breaking into an atmosphere that is teaching us the importance of music, then goes.

Now Di brings it all together. All the groups play a theme at once, what Di calls a basic shape. The topic is Greece, and this is the Minotaur theme. Ensemble repetitions of this theme are sandwiched among each group's composition. Di conducts the room through the whole piece.

Later, she says, 'You have two minutes to think about your pentatonic theme. What does that mean? What else has 'pent' in it? What do you think it means?' They talk among themselves, then sing, quite unselfconsciously:

CEGGAAG
CCED
CCEEDDG
DDEC

I ask Jamie about his instrument (it turns out to be a chanter) but he is too anxious about missing anything Di says and therefore making a mistake to answer, so I leave him. They sing:

Theseus killed the Minotaur
Long long ago
Tied the thread up to the door
Long long ago

and Di says 'That's good. We're all together. We're together so we're safe! It's when we're alone that there's danger. It doesn't matter if we make mistakes, everyone makes mistakes.'

Di is very much in control. When she asks about the pentatonic scale, she says 'I'll wait till everybody's hand is up ... it doesn't matter what you say, have a go. Come on – music isn't a doddle, it's hard work.' She gives music an authority in this classroom that I've rarely seen it given before and I wonder if the parents share her enthusiasm: that woman, for example, with the more urgent concern with the door key, these people I can glimpse from the hall window, shopping in St Helen's Street, across the other side of the graveyard.

This is Ipswich's equivalent of an inner city school, with no grass and lots of corridor and stairs, and it is hard not to rejoice that these children have this astonishing richness. I'd love to know if the parents rejoice too, but there is no time to find out. Even books, I am discovering, have deadlines. The deadline for this one approaches, and there's still an editor to convince. I look at the houses, huddled outside, and make a note to find out what the people there think.

Outside a group of younger children are having a games lesson, tossing plastic pink balls in twos. A teacher in an anorak with a whistle in her mouth hugs herself against the wind. Over the wall is the graveyard, and the roofs of terraced houses. Not that far away is County Hall, where the LEA responds to gradual but accelerating legislation leading to its eventual death. They often send visitors here, partly because of its convenience, but also because, despite its ugly setting, it's a very photogenic school, with its vivid art, its different ethnic groups. In the hall, the behaviour is excellent. The arts well taught have a sensitising influence, making heavy discipline unnecessary.

Di said to me later:

> Our school has worked towards an art policy for several years and we feel happy with what we've got at the moment and we're doing the same with the music. I collect instruments, and lots of these are mine, like those post horns, but we do spend money on expensive things as well, like that contrabass, it cost over a hundred pounds, but it's necessary if you're going to give them the quality. In so many ways children in schools are fobbed off with the second rate, but they get the best in music here. I teach them they can make music in so many ways. I'm very dubious about big productions because the most gifted of them get all the plum parts.

> Yes, I have a passion about the arts. I can get them to respond to beauty, it's necessary to make a complete person, to get to the soul. Of course I think the arts are threatened by the National Curriculum, but I'll go on doing them as long as I'm allowed, I'll give them their due with added enthusiasm while they're being downgraded, of course I will! I used to enjoy planning my teaching of an evening. I'd die if the last bit of creativity left to teaching went, if all I had to do was . . .

She shrugs. Perhaps she'd die if she became merely a hired hand delivering a centrally devised package.

> Yes. You can't educate the whole person if the arts aren't prominent, without them there's something enormous missing. Very often a child who isn't good at basic things, perhaps can't add up or is always lagging behind in some way in the academic work, can really shine in these subjects like music. I feel very strongly about that. I aim to give them a dictionary of techniques of art . . . to show them that, if they put everything into it, whatever they do, whatever anyone does, is valuable.

The lesson ends with something lighter: they sing and play:

Circle to the left the old brass wagon
Circle to the left the old brass wagon
Circle to the left the old brass wagon
You're the one my darling.

Later Di told me: 'I went on a course run by Wendy Bird, consultant for BBC programmes. She has an enthusiastic approach and we bought her books, introduced the course to the school.

We have two identical sets of instruments, one upstairs, one downstairs, kept in trolleys which are timetabled, everything is there, tapes, books, so if someone comes along who is rather unsure about music they've got that there as a firm structure. Everyone uses the instruments. Someone who is more confident can go to it now and then.

'We made instruments. A father brought in a lot of metal objects and one of the songs the littlies sing is called The Metal Man, and so my class made some metal instruments and then we tried them out to the song of The Metal Man and we've put them in the trolley as extras.'

Unusual school, St Helen's. It has one basic set of instruments upstairs, one set downstairs, and it has a contrabass costing a hundred pounds. If there is anywhere where the non-vocational, the non-cost-effective is central it's here. Someone is keeping the temple clean of money-changers – but for how long? I think of the huddled houses, and what they think of it all, and what they deserve, and don't get.

Notes Towards a Conclusion

A rabbi went to a wicked city to preach: first, about the goodness of God, and, second, against the sins of the city. 'After all,' he mused, anticipating Dylan Thomas by a couple of millennia. 'I work for the pleasure of man and the glory of God.' If he worried about a contradiction there, it isn't recorded: after all, he wasn't a puritan. And had he anticipated the middle and late twentieth-century flowering of the women's movement, he would have said 'humankind' or something more imaginative than that, but he hadn't, and he didn't. He was stuck, as we all are, with his history.

Anyway, he went from group to group for days, weeks and months, years probably, speaking up for the search for the truth – understanding intermittently, like the student, the *child* he still was, that the search, as long as you mean it, *is* the truth.

A boy ran along behind him. After many days he tugged at the rabbi's sleeve. 'Mr ... Rabbi ... *teacher* ... Don't you see no-one is listening. Why do you go on speaking?'

'I know.'

'Then?'

'At first I thought I could change these people. Now I know I can't. But I go on speaking, in case they change me.'

Writers supporting the arts often use religious imagery because religion is one repository of non- or anti-materialistic thinking. They use the notion of faith as a metaphor and a safe haven: at least here we will be free of values that are concerned only with the cash nexus. 'The electorate,' someone wrote to me on 10 April 1992, 'can be bribed with a stale bun.' The resort to religion means essentially that we are looking for a world where such bribery is unthinkable, where the stale bun, the share offer, the Canary Wharf Tower (can *you* tell the difference?) matters

154

nothing. Where someone has understood again, after all this time, these two millennia, that the love of money is the root of all evil.

In the end, when the enemy possesses the field, the religious person and the artist go on talking in case they become philistines. Vilified perhaps as the chattering classes, they retain the language of the temple as it was before the money-changers got there. They are at one with Christ (if in no other way) in their anger.

The English politician has coolly managed (to use one of his [sic] keywords) the demise of the public sector of eduction to the point where schools survive without enough teachers and books, without the wherewithal to teach Shakespeare or physics properly. Short term monetary objectives have persuaded schools to dump all sorts of things that before had been considered necessary: artists in residence, books, pictures, videos of plays, musical recordings – and, in at least one school, (and you can be sure it will be a trend-setting one) a deputy head.

Some secondary schools work with money in the deposit account at the bank, but with each student sharing a textbook. Everyone familiar with the system knows this is true, but only some care. But it will be noticed by liberal cynics that the English politician has made sure none of the damage affects himself or his family: his children, by and large, go to private schools.

Art is about play. When I say play, I mean play in the sense of purposeful exploration. Children's play is always purposeful, except when contaminated by adult versions of reality: mass produced games, toys that reinforce stereotypes like Cindy dolls and He-men. These foreclose on the potential learning. They substitute for exploration an emotional and psychological template. With play children try out their imaginative ideas. Puritanism, stemming from Judaeo-Christian notions of original sin, and other sources about which I am ignorant, has an antipathy towards play, exploration and the secular arts.

Other fundamentalisms threaten the life of the world, or at least (at least?) the artistic and scientific aspects of it. One thinks of the attempted suppression of a novel by a kind of Islam; of the banning of the teaching of evolution by a rightwing, triumphalist Christianity in the USA. And different kinds of puritanism threaten, though not all of them are religious. An MP, for example, is quoted as saying in the TES for 13 December 1991: 'We are worried about the level of education [nursery] schools provide. They shouldn't just be about play.' But evidence surrounds us in schools that children learn most effectively through play. That when children are arranged in rows listening to a teacher, they learn in a constipated, moribund way.

The three vital components of early learning are first-hand experience, play and talk. And play is the vital component, because it is involved in both the others. Look, for a moment, at this two-year-old in dungarees. She is carrying a plastic spade from the lower to the upper part of the garden. This spade is full of earth. She has an expression on her face of earnest concentration: she knows what she is doing and why she is doing it. We, as adults, have only dim ideas, filtered through bored readings of Piaget and other lesser writers glimpsed in books and journals. Compared with this child, we are ignorant.

She drops the earth in a hole she's made previously. She stands, smells the earth, bends to pat it, feels it with her hands, slapping them on the flattened mud. She goes back to find more earth, smelling and looking at it on the way, weighing it in the spade at the end of her arms.

When children play they set up little realities, they question other big ones. They demand – and get for a moment – an autonomy. 'But I'm the doctor ... I'm doing this ... Look how this happens ...' They make up hypotheses about the nature of things: earth, spade, plastic, muscles. They are learning.

The educational area with hegemony at the moment is management, of whatever style. It's worth noting that books published before the mid-seventies with titles like *From Day to Day in the Primary School, The Curriculum of the Junior School, Handbook of Suggestions for the consideration of teachers* and *The Changing Primary School* never mention management. In Irene Serjeant's book from the fifties, for example, the chapter titles are: Young children at work; Children at work; Self-chosen work of children 6 and 7 years of age; Children at work and play: Association and co-operation; Free dramatic work; Recording experiences and ideas; The natural approach to reading and writing; Learning to read; Early work in number; Number toys for 5-year-old children; Number interests of children 6 to 7 years of age; Number related to everyday experiences; The daily programme.

In the 1980s, books which focused so steadily on children and their learning were marginalised: they were printed by fugitive presses. In contrast, a book on *The developing school* (Peter Holly and Geoff Southworth) published in 1989 has the following for chapters titles: The learning school; The developing school; Leadership in the developing primary school; Managing school development in the primary school; Evaluation for development; Staff development; School development; Making it happen.

I am not saying these notions are reprehensible. I am, though, asking what effect they have had, and will have in the future, on the teaching of the arts. The essential words of management are mechanistic: effective, efficiency, training, inputs, skills and investment. So over-managerial styles de-humanise. They also see sponsorship, for example, as unproblematical. But would a whisky manufacturer allow education about alcohol abuse? Is a record company likely to insist on its own records being used in music lessons and in assemblies? One head said to me: 'It's devils, supping and long spoons when it comes to sponsorship.'

Inside the school, the effects of an enterprise culture will naturally turn on notions of efficiency. Here again, experiment, which is the heart of artistic expression, is not necessarily an efficient way of going about schooling. Experiment, that plays and works with our tentative and negotiable views of the way the world is, takes longer than art that builds largely on previous examples. It uses rough drafts and a great deal more material, of course. And, most importantly, it constantly risks offence.

If the enterprise society is going to invest in schools, it is likely that the first kind of art – the inoffensive, the easier, the popular, the confirming (and my original mistype there, 'conforming' was a happy one), the unrevolutionary will be welcomed in schools, as it will not lose money. It won't send the parents away to a neighbouring school. It will, instead, rely on the deft daftness of a fashionable pop opera. It seems unlikely too that the Zeussian leader will support any art that might rock the ship of state.

I take the word 'Zeussian' from a book by Charles Handy, who wrote about four gods of management, the first of whom is Zeus, sitting in the middle of a spider's web, the threads of which communicate orders. (The other gods of management are work-oriented Apollo, experimental and careless Athena, and

Dionysus, the god of wine and song.) The question of the hero-innovator becomes serious, because he or she is unlikely to finance art that questions the order that he or she has formed. Zeus, or Juno, 'turns schools around'. The vigour of that phrase, speaking as it does of a giant wrestling with a recalcitrant institution, leaves little room for artistic experiment. Or anything else.

In extreme cases, art seen as subversive will actually be suppressed. But in most schools and colleges, the explicit suppression of art is not as significant as the changing of the atmosphere so that risk-taking art will not be tried. The experiments will not suit the climate, and will not happen; this is suppression just the same.

The British way of disempowering art though – that is, ignoring it – is even more likely to occur. This is what happens at Garth Hill. The book describing this school has plentiful index references to computers, CDT, business education and industry, and nothing on the arts except two little mentions of music – the one art we can use in an image-conscious way to impress parents and the invited representatives of local industry: the one art that puts a public face on without risk, because usually it has no words and no actions interpretable in a literal way, as do, on the other hand, dance, narrative, poetry, and theatre.

And this ignoring, and subtle changing of the atmosphere to an anti-experimental one, is no less dangerous than the activities of the neo-fascist hero-innovator, whether he is an Ayatollah, an American evangelical, or some other puritan, who goes around censoring programmes, burning books or banning suspect productions because of the sexual orientation of the writer.

Below is an example of a school seduced by a task-oriented, Apollonian management style: A.....-shire school uses the following piece of paper headed **English Department Third Year Study of Poetry**. It 'consists of a menu of statements selected by the school from the 'Assessment Profile in English' statement book:

NAME:

has shown the ability to:

1 Compose simple, formal rhymes, e.g. limericks.

2 Recognise figurative language (find images or word pictures, e.g. metaphor, simile, personification).
3 Explain the use of figurative language (say how and why figurative language is being used).
4 Compose his/her own effective similes and metaphors.
5 Identify poetic techniques (e.g. use of rhyme, rhythm, alliteration, verse layout).
6 Show understanding of why particular poetic techniques have been chosen.
7 Experiment with poetic techniques (take 'risks' with techniques).
8 Use poetic techniques where and as appropriate.
9 Share the feelings or mood of a poet.
10 Express an overall view of a poet's intention.
11 Read poetry with expression, paying attention to rhythm and meaning.
12 Relate the content of a poem to own personal experience.
13 Draft and re-draft (write, change and re-write).

Now the National Curriculum Council wrote in 1989 (the Cox Report):

> The best writing is vigorous, committed, honest and interesting. We have not included these qualities in our attainment targets because they cannot be mapped on to levels.

Management is not the substantive issue in any school worthy of the name. The substantive issue is education: the moment between a person – a child, probably, but also, sometimes, a teacher, a parent or a governor – not understanding something ... and their understanding it, or beginning to understand it. Management is merely (yes, merely) an enabling mechanism, and the quieter that mechanism the better. Like all mechanisms it has a low status, especially compared with the substantive issue: the transformation, the temporary stay against confusion that education, that art, offer.

And it is also true that the school where the teachers share these moments is the stronger school, the educational school. Where, on the other hand, teachers are controlled with the adding up of columns of figures, the drawing up of meaningless plans on what Causley calls 'useless bits of paper', and negotiations about sponsorship with The Acme Brush Co. Ltd. – these are the poor schools, the essentially un- or even anti-educational ones.

If you want art and you want education, you'd better begin plotting against Zeus, whatever form he takes: bull, swan, shower of gold, philistine government. Apollo and Athena will be easier to subvert. Only Dionysus will set the imagination free.

The.....-shire document – which has three boxes for ticks after each objective – is an attempt to do the impossible: that is, to chart the affective powers of poetry and our responses to it. It is an example of what a system will do in its attempt to put everything in order: in so doing it will, inevitably, falsify human experience. Philip Larkin wrote that 'where desire takes charge, readings will grow erratic'. In fact, as long as humanity is calling the tune, systematic readings are always unreliable at best, and downright falsifying at worst: as here. Indeed, it is not really the artist who is Dionysian, but human nature in all its unpredictability.

The managerial insistence on effectiveness and end-results, objectives and targets, measurement and competitiveness, has brought some teachers to an absurd position where they are working to instructions that bounce insanely from the relatively simple ('Identify ... rhyme') to the extremely difficult ('Show an understanding of why particular poetic techniques have been chosen') and then to the existentially impossible ('Share the feelings or mood of a poet').

The tension between the exploratory function of art, and the need to measure and categorise, is uncomfortably evident. Who says what is 'effective'? So many questions are begged. After 6 one wants to ask, does a poet choose a technique at all? How does one 'show an understanding'? After 8 one wants to know who is to decide whether a particular technique is appropriate – after all, one of Larkin's most celebrated poems, 'The Explosion', about a pit disaster (in *High Windows* 1977), is written in the metre of 'Hiawatha'. A conventional view about appropriateness in art would have blocked that poem. Any sense of the absurd is clearly missing from the writer's armoury, or he/she would not expect anyone to be able to 'express an overall view of a poet's intention'.

The roots of the thinking that produced this document are in the accountability rhetoric of the late seventies and the eighties. Obviously, teachers cannot be accountable for the invisible. Therefore the invisible must be made visible. Unfortunately (perhaps) and as the Cox Committee originally recognised, this is impossible. There is no correlation between vigour, honesty, commitment and interest on the one hand, and any recording system that depends on measurement.

The accountability rhetoric was accompanied by a management rhetoric that I have already analysed: training, enterprise and effectiveness. While Zeus and Apollo have the hegemony, there is no opportunity for the creative surprise.

How do we evaluate, or assess, the holiness of the heart's affections? Eight-year-old Clare has never been confident about writing. Today her teacher is away, and the supply teacher talks to her class about rivers, the topic she'd planned in her car as she responded to the eight-thirty phone call that morning. Now, the teacher talks about the rivers Orwell, Stour and Deben. The children remember sitting by them and fishing and throwing stones into them. They talk, in response to the teacher's questions, about what the light looks like on the water; about the creatures that live there. About rowing boats and weather, bridges and banks and mud and walks and ducks.

Then they talk about the Thames, which some of them have seen, and which some have sailed on. One child has seen the Shannon. The teacher tells a story about the Liffey. Eventually Clare writes:

The river

Morning has just come
Sunlight lay on the
water like a blanket
on a bed. a round
circle appears like
a ball. the ball is
the ball is the sun

The end

it is late the children
set of home the moon
was bright. it looks like
a lump cheese.

the end

by Clare

How do we assess that? We need, for a start, to think about Clare herself, and not just her poem. We will consider her character (rather timid, in classrooms, most of the time, but becoming more assertive, according to her teachers) and her learning styles. And it would help if we knew what the supply teacher said to Clare when she read the first 'the end', and what Clare replied, and how she felt about the teacher's comments. When you've got this information, we'll give you leave to make a provisional assessment of Clare's poem.

It took a lot out of her. Rivers turned her on one day, but why would anyone want to clap a measure on it? Numbers won't tell us the lucky number on which she wrote. Who knows the secret parts of Clare she brought to the piece of paper she scribbled on? Performance is a pitiful epithet for this poem, for any poem, for Clare's learning, for all our pupils' learning. We can – and will – do better.

Or how do we assess the work described in any of these chapters?

Almost the last words belong to children: Tulani is 11, Chloe 8, Edward 11, Barry 10 and Daniel 10.

What's the most important subject you have at school?

T The most important subject is art. I don't know why. It just is.

E It's an interesting subject, art, I get jarred off with maths, you have to do what you are told, with art you can do what you like, you make your own ideas and work on them. Drawing is better than writing, writing takes too long and it's boring, in maths you just get set things to do.

B I agree you get jarred off with maths and that but I'm not sure art is more important than maths and English because you need them when you grow up for a job don't you, degrees and that. Qualifications. You gotta get a job, you gotta have maths and English, art's not so important, it's not so important for getting a job anyway.

C English is the most important subject. With English, you have to work them, the words, out for yourself. In English if you get the words wrong he doesn't get angry with you, he just corrects them.

D Poetry. I enjoy doing it. Maybe it won't get me a *full-time* job. But I like poetry best.

Is writing an art?

T Poetry is art*ish*. English isn't kind of art 'cos you can write about anything in poetry, but in language you have to copy out of a book, comprehension, you know, all that stuff, and it's boring. Poetry's art.

E Poetry is definitely art, definitely, you don't have to make up a story, you put any old words down, you can picture it, poetry, in your head. Some poetry is really weird, silly rhymes and nonsense. In stories you can't picture it, it's just everyday life. Ordinary. Poetry is normally about . . . well, animals, colours, shapes, pictures.

D Poetry is not trying to rhyme all the time!

B Poetry is more powerful than stories, I mean with poetry the words give you a feeling, a picture.

D Poetry is art and some stories are too. Comics aren't art.

E Yes it is because it's drawing and there are dedicated comics, art is just doing something well as you can, making an art of it, being dedicated, you know.

B I agree with Daniel, comics are not really art, they're cartoons which don't give you a good picture of what's going on.

D Sometimes Roald Dahl is art, sometimes he isn't. He's too comic-y sometimes. Like in Charlie, that's a bit comic-y. Danny is the most artistic book by Roald Dahl.

B I don't like dance much. I don't know why. It's jarring. But I suppose it's good for your health!

E That's games, Barry!

B And dance. Dance is good for your health. But I don't like it much. No.

D Dance isn't my sort of thing really. And I don't like plays and stuff, I like it on the night, yeah, when the audience is there, that's okay, but I don't like all the practising. We did drama in class last year. We did silent pictures. There was a man in and he told us a story and we had to make ten silent pictures for that story. We did a man on a boat, he'd gone out to look for some treasure and he was going back on a rowing boat, and we had two people on each side for the boat and someone was an oar and someone was sitting in the boat.

T Well I *like* practising. I like it when you can change the bits about and next time you'll be able to say 'Well, this is how we done it last time.' And I think dance is good because you get to work with other people. Miss Martino says [teacherly voice] 'Get into mixed groups, get into mixed groups, different age groups . . . Come on, no arguing, chop chop'. You get to know each other, it's easier to work with other people. I like working in groups in drama, too.

C I prefer working on my own because you don't get ideas from other people. When you have your own ideas they fit together, but in a group some fit and some don't, you have to decide which ones to write down and do and which ones not to write down and do.

E I like working by myself. You can put your own ideas down. If you've done something by yourself, it's more satisfying, you don't have to say 'John did that bit, Edward did that bit, Anthony did that bit.'

T I like groups. You get to know how people like to work, you get ideas from other people. But it's true, it does lead to arguments sometimes, that's true.

EVERYONE Yes. Yes it does. Arguments.

D I like working in a group because I feel more secure. You're more likely to get it right. If you get it wrong it's easier to do it again and get it right. Maths. It's easier working together. But you can't write poems in groups, it just can't be done. Dance is best done in groups, you can make more shapes like.

Is dance an art?

D It's art because it's kind of making shapes with your body, like in poetry, the lines, how short the lines are, and long. And painting, most of painting is about shapes.

E Most things are an art if you're good at them. That's what I'm saying. Make an art of it, them, like fishing. If you do a difficult thing well that's art. Yes, even nuclear physics.

How would you describe earth art to a Martian?

T Lots of colours. You need imagination. You can think of things inside your head and put them on paper . . . Yes, or in a dance, in a poem, in a play.

B All education is really art.

C They all have a thing that somebody likes so they consider that thing art.

D Art is being good at something.

E If you do a really clever murder – a really clever murder, a *really* clever one – like on Colombo the other week, this man shot his wife, but there was all these bangs from the record player and there was a firework display so nobody knew about the gun noise – that was clever. That is art.

D No that's not right. 'Cos art's not horrible. I did this picture once of my rabbit playing in a one-man band. My mum and dad liked it, but I don't know if it was art.

PASSING TEACHER Emily [her 13-year-old daughter] would say art is what you can do, science is what you can't.

C My favourite art is normal art, collages and that. I prefer looking at other art, seeing how people do it, seeing how they think. Comparing it to how you think.

E Poetry. I'd have to say poetry. And scenery pictures. Those ones made out of dots.

D My favourite art is screen printing. It's just fun. I quite like the mess, but that's not why I like it!

T I prefer making my own. When I was in the infants, I can think back on it, what I did, and see you've . . . I've improved. I like doing that.

E That's looking at art as well!

D So do I. I like both. Looking at other people's can provide entertainment – well, they both can, but things like football, I like watching that, that's art if it's good, if the players are good and everything, yeah, that's art then.

B I prefer making my own. You can learn from making mistakes, but you can't learn from other people's art.

E You can! My favourite artist is Beethoven. No. That bloke who sings The Four Seasons, you know, who's that bloke?

C Vivaldi.

E What?

C That's Vivaldi.

B My favourite artist . . . I think it has to be a visual artist. I think . . . I think . . . Michelangelo. He did that chapel, what's it called. He nearly always does gods and spirits and people. I like him. My favourite record has to be The Drifters' Greatest Hits.

T I don't know much about artists, except Picasso. He does the strange pictures. I know some people don't like them, but I do. They're *different*. He used strange colours. And who's that artist who tore up paper? I like him. Yeah, Matisse. He's different as well.

C Van Gogh.

E He was mad!

B (to E) So are you!

EVERYONE EXCEPT E Yeah!

C His pictures . . . I like them, very much. He puts all the little lines into the paints with different colours, makes it look . . . exotic. And if he was doing a picture like this [points at a poster] he'd put in lots of details, I like details. All the paint'd run together and make it all look nice. He makes everyday things look different, *exotic!*

B I like that one who did all the little dots.

E I like Quentin Blake.

T I like Judy Blume.

D I like Chuck Berry. He's not soppy and slow and he's not sort of madly fast. I like 'No Particular Place To Go' best. I like Dickens and Tolkien.

C I like Enid Blyton.

As the deadline approaches – and passes – I worry about the rabbi that I heard about as I began these notes towards a conclusion. There's a sanctimonious air about him. I don't want to be like them, he's saying. I'm better. And that is the cry of the evangelist and Pharisee, however it's been masked, down the ages. But this book is about a more frightening worry, that goes some way towards excusing sanctimony, a nightmare we wouldn't have thought on the boundaries of possibility twenty years ago. It's about the marginalisation of the arts, so they're not in the core of the curriculum, but on the edge; barely, in many cases, in the schools at all.

At the end of this nightmare, as the arts disappear, bullied by censorship and sponsorship, the twin requirements of a nervy capitalist triumphalism and its inevitable friend, big business, so democracy goes. In 1980 an elderly poet said to me about the new government: 'They will destroy the intellectuals and the working classes' and I said, you're over the top, it's not that bad, they won't. Now the arts are in the doghouse, and the new working class is an underclass in cardboard boxes, and he was spot on. And the arts have to battle, not just for themselves, but for everybody who knows that his or her right to speak is threatened.

References

Throughout
National Curriculum and SEAC documents, 1989–1992.
Lawrence Stenhouse (1976) *An Introduction to Curriculum Design and Development* Heinemann.
Roland Barthes (1982) *A Barthes Reader* ed. Sontag, Cape.

Introduction
John Cotton (1986) *Daybook* Priapus Press.
Louis MacNeice (1966) *Collected Poems* Faber.
Fred Sedgwick (1986) 'Chipping at the Monolith' in *Curriculum* 7/2.
Deirdre Bair (1990) *Samuel Beckett: A biography* Vintage.
David Constantine, from 'Letters to Mrs Thatcher and Mr Kinnock', *Guardian* 15 August 1990.
AMMA Report *The Arts* 1990.
Denys Thompson (ed.) (1969) *Directions* CUP.
Morag Styles *et al.* (1992) *After Alice* Cassell.
F R Leavis (1930) *Mass Civilisation and Minority Culture* Chatto and Windus.
Peter Abbs (1986) *Living Powers* Falmer.
Mary Jane Drummond (1993) *Assessing Children's Learning* David Fulton.
Jeremy Robson (1975) *Poetry Dimension* Abacus.
Contemporary Poets 5th Edition (1991) St James Press.

Chapter 1
Vernon Scannell (1977) *A Proper Gentleman* Robson Books.
Francis Stillman (1966) *Poet's Manual and Rhyming Dictionary* Thames and Hudson.
Fred Sedgwick (1988) 'The Sifter's Story' *Cambridge Journal of*

Education 18/1.
Sandy Brownjohn (1980) *Does It Have to Rhyme?* Hodder and Stoughton.
Frank Smith (1982) *Writing and the Writer* Heinemann.
Jill Pirrie (1987) *On Common Ground* Hodder and Stoughton.
Robert Hull (1988) *Behind the Poem* Routledge.
W H Auden (1992) *Collected Poems* Faber.
Fred Sedgwick (1989) *Here Comes the Assembly Man* Falmer.
Seamus Heaney (1979) *Fieldwork* Faber.
' ... not all lead and fluospar ...' (1991) *Stories and poems from Weardale* Northern Voices.

Chapter 2
W H Auden, *A Certain World* Faber. (The St Augustine quotation)
Angela Huth (1987) *Island of the Children* Orchard.
Hans Magnus Enzenberger (1989) *The Sinking of the Titanic* Paladin.
Alec Clegg (1965) *The Excitement of Writing* Chatto and Windus.
Fred Sedgwick (1989) *This Way That Way* Mary Glasgow Publications.

Chapter 3
John Lancaster (1990) *Art in the Primary School* Routledge.
John Rowe Townsend (1971) *Modern Poetry* OUP.

Chapter 4
Mary Newland and Maurice Rubens (1983) *Some Functions of Art in the Primary School* ILEA.
Calouste Gulbenkian Foundation (1982) *The Arts in Schools*.

Chapter 5
James Berry (1988) *When I Dance* Puffin.
Les Tickle (1987) *The Arts in Education* Croom Helm.
Peter Abbs (1987) *Living Powers* Falmer.
Seamus Heaney (1966) *Death of a Naturalist* Faber.

Chapter 6
Fred Sedgwick (1988) 'Talking about Teaching Poetry' *Curriculum* 9/3.
Mary Lowden (1986) *Dancing to Learn* Falmer.

Sue Harrison (1988) 'Assessment in Dance', Fourth International Conference ...

Chapter 7
Les Tickle (1987) *The Arts in Education* Croom Helm.
Kit Wright (1989) *Cat Among the Pigeons* Kestrel.
Gareth Owen (ed.) (1987) *School's Out* OUP.

Chapter 8
Stanley Goodchild and Peter Holly (1989) *Management for Change: The Garth Hill Experience* Falmer.

Notes Towards a Conclusion
Irene Serjeant (1952) *From Day to Day in the Infant School* Blackie.
National Union of Teachers (1958) *The Curriculum of the Junior School* NUT.
Board of Education (1937) *Handbook of Suggestions for Teachers* HMSO.
Peter Holly and Geoff Southworth (1989) *The Developing School* Falmer.

Index

170